MATH
POWER PACKS
◎ Reproducible Homework Packets ◎

Published by

Frank Schaffer
Publications®
Columbus, Ohio

Frank Schaffer Publications®

Send all inquiries to:
Frank Schaffer Publications
8720 Orion Place
Columbus, Ohio 43240-2111

Math Power Packs—Grade 4

ISBN 0-7682-3494-8

2 3 4 5 6 7 8 9 10 GLO 12 11 10 09

Table of Contents

Letter to Teacher 4

Math Vocabulary List 5

Math Standards Scoring Rubric 6–7

What's Happening This Month 8

Power Pack: Number Concepts—Whole Numbers 9–19

Power Pack: Number Concepts—
        Fractions, Decimals, and Percents 20–30

Power Pack: Addition and Subtraction 31–41

Power Pack: Multiplication and Division 42–52

Power Pack: Measurement—Linear Measurement,
        Area, and Volume 53–63

Power Pack: Measurement—Capacity, Mass,
        Time, and Temperature 64–74

Power Pack: Algebra 75–85

Power Pack: Geometry 86–96

Power Pack: Data Analysis and Probability 97–107

Power Pack: Problem Solving 108–118

Answer Key 119–128

Dear Teacher,

We realize that extra homework practice is sometimes necessary for student success. *Math Power Packs* alleviate some of your heavy workload by providing ready-made homework packets right at your fingertips!

The packets in this book cover the six essential strands of mathematics—number and operations, measurement, algebra, geometry, data and probability, and problem solving—that are tested on standardized assessments. The packets were carefully crafted to meet national state standards and NCTM standards for school mathematics. To ensure that your students understand these important principles, a reproducible scoring rubric is included.

Each packet comes with a customizable cover letter to parents and ten activity sheets. All you have to do is fill in the appropriate information on the cover sheet for each packet, photocopy the reproducible pages, and send them home with your students. We recommend that you use these homework packets to reinforce the topics you are covering in the classroom. Send each packet home to give students further opportunities to practice skills, to help teach them responsibility, and to encourage independent work.

The home-school connection is an important one. To help strengthen and encourage rapport with your students' parents and guardians, we've included a blank calendar template. Use this to inform parents of homework due dates, upcoming quizzes and tests, and special events. There is an "additional notes to parents" section on each cover sheet that allows you to write specific notes and concerns home. You can also photocopy the math vocabulary sheet included in the book to send home so that parents fully understand the terms and concepts their children are practicing.

We trust that *Math Power Packs* will be a rewarding addition to your classroom. By utilizing the ready-made packets in this series, you are providing students with the extra learning power necessary for school success!

Sincerely,
Frank Schaffer Publications

Math Vocabulary List

acute—angle measuring less than 90 degrees

area—the amount of surface within a certain space

associative property—in an addition or multiplication problem, the numbers can be grouped in any way and the answer will remain the same

commutative property—changing the position of the numbers in an addition or multiplication problem does not change the answer

congruent—having the same size and shape

distributive property—the property where multiplication is applied to the addition of two or more numbers. Each term inside a set of parentheses can be multiplied by a factor outside the parentheses. Example: a (b + c) = ab + ac

edge—the place where two faces of a solid figure meet

equilateral triangle—a triangle with three equal sides

face—a flat surface of a solid figure

fact family—three numbers that are related and make a set of related math facts

factor—a number multiplied by another number; a value that goes into a number evenly without remainders

inverse operations—two operations that have the opposite effect of one another

isosceles triangle—a triangle with two equal sides

least common multiple—the smallest nonzero number that is a multiple of two or more numbers

line segment—a specific portion of a line with two endpoints

mean—the average of a group of numbers

median—the number in the middle when a group of numbers is put in order

minuend—a number from which another is subtracted

mode—the number, or item, that you see most often in a set

obtuse—angle measuring more than 90 degrees

outlier—a value not typical of the other values in a set

parallelogram—a flat, closed figure with four sides and opposite sides parallel

percent—a number, followed by the % symbol, indicating how many out of 100 equal parts

perimeter—the total distance around a shape

point symmetry—a figure that can be turned 360 degrees on a point and remain the same

prime number—a number whose only factors are 1 and itself

prism—three-dimensional shape with two identical polygon bases and rectangular faces

product—the result of two or more numbers being multiplied together

pyramid—three-dimensional shape with a polygon base, triangular faces, and a point on one end

quadrilateral—a flat, closed figure with four sides

range—the difference between the greatest number and the least number in a data set

ray—a figure that goes on forever in one direction from a fixed end point

right—angle measuring 90 degrees

scalene triangle—a triangle with three unequal sides

subtrahend—a number that is subtracted from another number

symmetrical—a figure that has two congruent halves

variable—a letter used to represent a number value

volume—the amount of space inside a three-dimensional figure

Math Standards Scoring Rubric

1 = Does Not Meet **2 = Somewhat Meets** **3 = Meets** **4 = Somewhat Exceeds** **5 = Exceeds**

Number and Operations

Understands numbers, ways of representing numbers, relationships among numbers, and number systems.

	understands the place-value structure of the base-ten number system and can represent and compare whole numbers and decimals
	recognizes equivalent representations for the same number and generates them by decomposing and composing numbers
	develops understanding of fractions as parts of unit wholes, as parts of a collection, as locations on number lines, and as divisions of whole numbers
	uses models, benchmarks, and equivalent forms to judge the size of fractions
	recognizes and generates equivalent forms of commonly used fractions, decimals, and percents
	explores numbers less than 0 by extending the number line and through familiar applications
	describes classes of numbers according to characteristics, such as the nature of their factors

Understands meanings of operations and how they relate to one another.

	understands various meanings of multiplication and division
	understands the effects of multiplying and dividing whole numbers
	identifies and uses relationships between operations, such as division as the inverse of multiplication, to solve problems
	understands and uses properties of operations, such as the distributivity of multiplication over addition

Computes fluently and makes reasonable estimates.

	develops fluency with basic number combinations for multiplication and division and uses these combinations to mentally compute related problems, such as 30 x 50
	develops fluency in adding, subtracting, multiplying, and dividing whole numbers
	develops and uses strategies to estimate the results of whole-number computations and to judge the reasonableness of such results
	develops and uses strategies to estimate computations involving fractions and decimals in situations relevant to students' experience
	uses visual models, benchmarks, and equivalent forms to add and subtract commonly used fractions and decimals
	selects appropriate methods and tools for computing with whole numbers from among mental computation, estimation, calculators, and paper and pencil according to the context and nature of the computation and uses the selected method or tools

Algebra

Understands patterns, relations, and functions.

	describes, extends, and makes generalizations about geometric and numeric patterns
	represents and analyzes patterns and functions using words, tables, and graphs

Represents and analyzes mathematical situations and structures using algebraic symbols.

	identifies such properties as commutativity, associativity, and distributivity and uses them to compute with whole numbers
	represents the idea of a variable as an unknown quantity using a letter or a symbol
	expresses mathematical relationships using equations

Uses mathematical models to represent and understand quantitative relationships.

	models problem situations with objects and uses representations, such as graphs, tables, and equations, to draw conclusions

Analyzes change in various contexts.

	investigates how a change in one variable relates to a change in a second variable
	identifies and describes situations with constant or varying rates of change and compares them

Geometry

Analyzes characteristics and properties of two- and three-dimensional geometric shapes and develops mathematical arguments about geometric relationships.

	identifies, compares, and analyzes attributes of two- and three-dimensional shapes and develops vocabulary to describe the attributes
	classifies two- and three-dimensional shapes according to their properties and develops definitions of classes of shapes, such as triangles and pyramids
	investigates, describes, and reasons about the results of subdividing, combining, and transforming shapes
	explores congruence and similarity
	makes and tests conjectures about geometric properties and relationships and develops logical arguments to justify conclusions

Specifies locations and describes spatial relationships using coordinate geometry and other representational systems.

	describes location and movement using common language and geometric vocabulary
	makes and uses coordinate systems to specify locations and to describe paths
	finds the distance between points along horizontal and vertical lines of a coordinate system

Applies transformations and uses symmetry to analyze mathematical situations.

	predicts and describes the results of sliding, flipping, and turning two-dimensional shapes
	describes a motion or a series of motions that will show that two shapes are congruent
	identifies and describes line and rotational symmetry in two- and three-dimensional shapes and designs

Uses visualization, spatial reasoning, and geometric modeling to solve problems.

	builds and draws geometric objects
	creates and describes mental images of objects, patterns, and paths
	identifies and builds a three-dimensional object from two-dimensional representations of that object
	identifies and draws a two-dimensional representation of a three-dimensional object
	uses geometric models to solve problems in other areas of mathematics, such as number and measurement
	recognizes geometric ideas and relationships and applies them to other disciplines and to problems that arise in the classroom or in everyday life

Measurement

Understands measurable attributes of objects and the units, systems, and processes of measurement.

	understands such attributes as length, area, weight, volume, and size of angle and selects the appropriate type of unit for measuring each attribute
	understands the need for measuring with standard units and becomes familiar with standard units in the customary and metric systems
	carries out simple unit conversions, such as from centimeters to meters, within a system of measurement
	understands that measurements are approximations and how differences in units affect precision
	explores what happens to measurements of a two-dimensional shape, such as its perimeter and area, when the shape is changed in some way

Applies appropriate techniques, tools, and formulas to determine measurements.

	develops strategies for estimating the perimeters, areas, and volumes of irregular shapes
	selects and applies appropriate standard units and tools to measure length, area, volume, weight, time, temperature, and the size of angles
	selects and uses benchmarks to estimate measurements
	develops, understands, and uses formulas to find the area of rectangles and related triangles and parallelograms
	develops strategies to determine the surface areas and volumes of rectangular solids

Data Analysis and Probability

Formulates questions that can be addressed with data and collects, organizes, and displays relevant data to answer them.

	designs investigations to address a question and considers how data-collection methods affect the nature of the data set
	collects data using observations, surveys, and experiments
	represents data using tables and graphs, such as line plots, bar graphs, and line graphs
	recognizes the differences in representing categorical and numerical data

Selects and uses appropriate statistical methods to analyze data.

	describes the shape and important features of a set of data and compares related data sets with an emphasis on how the data are distributed
	uses measures of center, focusing on the median, and understands what each does and does not indicate about the data set
	compares different representations of the same data and evaluates how well each representation shows important aspects of the data

Develops and evaluates inferences and predictions that are based on data.

	proposes and justifies conclusions and predictions that are based on data and designs studies to further investigate the conclusions or predictions

Understands and applies basic concepts of probability.

	describes events as likely or unlikely and discusses the degree of likelihood using such words as *certain*, *equally likely*, and *impossible*
	predicts the probability of outcomes of simple experiments and tests the predictions
	understands that the measure of the likelihood of an event can be represented by a number from 0 to 1

Problem Solving

	builds new mathematical knowledge through problem solving
	solves problems that arise in mathematics and in other contexts
	applies and adapts a variety of appropriate strategies to solve problems
	monitors and reflects on the process of mathematical problem solving

What's Happening This Month

SUNDAY	MONDAY	TUESDAY	WEDNESDAY	THURSDAY	FRIDAY	SATURDAY

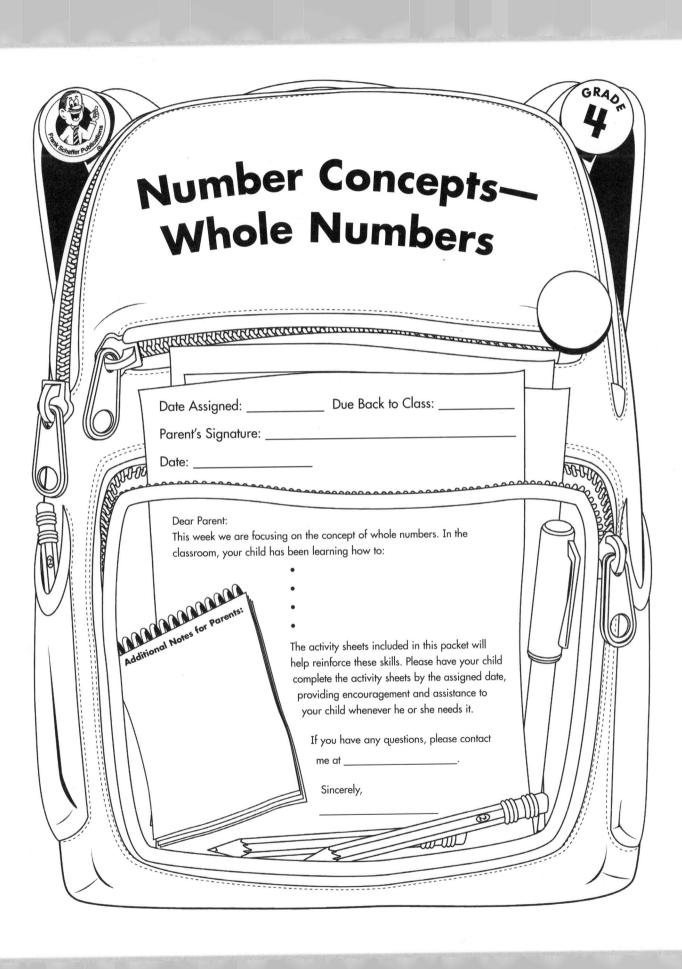

Number Concepts— Whole Numbers

GRADE 4

Date Assigned: _____ Due Back to Class: _____

Parent's Signature: _____

Date: _____

Additional Notes for Parents:

Dear Parent:

This week we are focusing on the concept of whole numbers. In the classroom, your child has been learning how to:

-
-
-

The activity sheets included in this packet will help reinforce these skills. Please have your child complete the activity sheets by the assigned date, providing encouragement and assistance to your child whenever he or she needs it.

If you have any questions, please contact me at _____.

Sincerely,

_____

Place Value

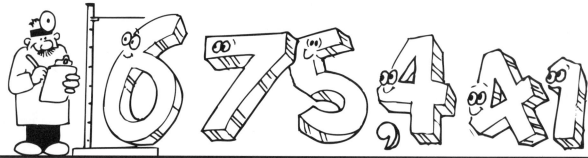

Hundred Thousands	Ten Thousands	Thousands	Hundreds	Tens	Ones
6	7	5	4	4	1
675,441					

Draw a line to match the numbers with the words. The first one has been done for you.

1. 54,671   one hundred thousand

2. 354,942   seven thousands

3. 203,203   two hundred thousands

4. 67,881   nine hundreds

5. 495,463   six tens

6. 485,751   five ones

7. 763,389   three hundreds

8. 892,855   eight ten thousands

9. 103,254   seven tens

Pull It Apart

Write the expanded form of each standard number.

Example:	5,407 = 5,000 + 400 + 7	**Thousands** **Hundreds**

1. 3,271,389 = _____

2. 5,504,928 = _____

3. 604,545 = _____

4. 241 = _____

5. 487,689 = _____

6. 34,900 = _____

7. 1,162 = _____

8. 940,761 = _____

9. 8,921,260 = _____

10. 753 = _____

Power Practice

On another sheet of paper, write each number on this page in word form.

Missing Information

Fill in the missing information.

1. word form: five thousand, four hundred thirteen

   standard form:

   expanded form:

   circle one: even or odd

2. word form:

   standard form: 2,568

   expanded form:

   circle one: even or odd

3. word form:

   standard form:

   expanded form: 7,000 + 500 + 2

   circle one: even or odd

4. word form: three thousand, two hundred eighty-one

   standard form:

   expanded form:

   circle one: even or odd

5. word form:

   standard form: 2,085

   expanded form:

   circle one: even or odd

Comparisons

When numbers are compared, they can be greater than (**>**), less than (**<**), or equal to (**=**). Place the correct symbol between each set of numbers.

1. 2,635	☐	2,689	**11.** 436,902	☐	543,902
2. 632,457	☐	700,016	**12.** 4,683,173	☐	4,628,137
3. 3,252,390	☐	3,252,390	**13.** 240,632	☐	230,698
4. 8,254	☐	8,245	**14.** 436	☐	905
5. 2,664	☐	627	**15.** 8,332	☐	20,191
6. 91	☐	71	**16.** 672	☐	547
7. 615	☐	1,002	**17.** 44,269	☐	44,269
8. 4,732,063	☐	4,573,064	**18.** 841	☐	795
9. 19,154	☐	19,952	**19.** 36	☐	42
10. 810	☐	698	**20.** 46,173	☐	102,114

Power Practice

Record your answers in a tally chart on a separate sheet of paper. Make one tally each time you use a symbol.

Name _____

The Next Number Is . . .

Intervals on number lines vary. Determine the next three numbers on the number line. Explain your answers.

1.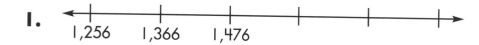
1,256   1,366   1,476

Explanation: _____

2.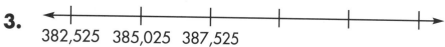
34,562   34,462   34,362

Explanation: _____

3.
382,525 385,025 387,525

Explanation: _____

4.
900,245 1,000,245 1,100,245

Explanation: _____

5.
569,352   568,352   567,352

Explanation: _____

Power Practice

Start with 500. Choose an interval. Make your own number line. Explain your number choices.

500

Explanation: _____

Rounding

Round each number to the underlined digit.

1. 4<u>7</u>6

_____

2. 1<u>2</u>4

_____

3. 9<u>0</u>5

_____

4. 124,<u>5</u>26

_____

5. 72,1<u>9</u>3

_____

6. 4,<u>5</u>27,686

_____

7. 7<u>4</u>,385

_____

8. 4,<u>3</u>25,961

_____

9. 152,<u>6</u>10

_____

10. 5,<u>8</u>36,351

_____

11. <u>4</u>26,318

_____

12. 2,9<u>3</u>7,518

_____

13. 1,645,<u>2</u>77

_____

14. 687,<u>0</u>23

_____

15. 2,672,<u>5</u>41

_____

16. 3<u>6</u>,513

_____

17. 3,6<u>7</u>8,282

_____

18. 8,032,<u>5</u>39

_____

19. <u>6</u>,734

_____

20. 2,<u>1</u>34,743

_____

21. 3,8<u>4</u>1,605

_____

22. 248,<u>9</u>67

_____

23. <u>3</u>5,721

_____

24. <u>1</u>,092,362

_____

The Right Place

You can write a number different ways.

Millions			Thousands			Ones		
Hundreds	Tens	Ones	Hundreds	Tens	Ones	Hundreds	Tens	Ones
2	9	0	7	3	4	6	0	0

Standard form: 290,734,600

Word form: two hundred ninety million, seven hundred thirty-four thousand, six hundred

Expanded form: 200,000,000 + 90,000,000 + 700,000 + 30,000 + 4,000 + 600

Answer each riddle by using each digit only once.

1 2 3 4 5 6 7 8 9

1. I am the greatest 9-digit number with 4 in the hundred millions place.

   <u>4</u> __ __, __ __ __, __ __ __

2. I am the least 9-digit number with 4 in the hundred millions place.

   __ __ __, __ __ __, __ __ __

3. I am the greatest 9-digit number with 8 in the ten thousands place.

   __ __ __, __ __ __, __ __ __

4. I am the least 9-digit number possible.

   __ __ __, __ __ __, __ __ __

5. I am the greatest 9-digit number with 7 in the ten thousands place and 1 in the hundreds place.

   __ __ __, __ __ __, __ __ __

Finding Factors

> A **factor** of a number is any value that goes into the number evenly (no remainders).

There are several "tricks" for finding factors of large numbers. You may be familiar with some of them already.

1. Complete the following statements.

   a. A number will have a factor of 2 if _____

   b. A number will have a factor of 5 if _____

   c. A number will have a factor of 10 if _____.

2. List the multiples of 3 up to 100. Find the sum of the digits in each multiple of 3. What do you notice?

3. List the multiples of 9 up to 100. Find the sum of the digits in each multiple of 9. What do you notice?

4. *Trick: A number will have a factor of 4 if 4 is a factor of the last 2 digits of the number.* Which of the following numbers have a factor of 4? Use the "trick." Then, test the trick. Divide each of the numbers by 4. Does the "trick" work for each number?

   128   2,464   272   346   388   2,300   718   4,512

Multiples

The multiples of 6 as far as 6 x 9 are:
6, 12, 18, 24, 30, 36, 42, 48, and 54.

The multiples of 9 as far as 9 x 9 are:
9, 18, 27, 36, 45, 54, 72, and 81.

Some of the multiples of 6 and 9 are alike. The numbers 18, 36, and 54 are common multiples of 6 and 9. Since 18 is the smallest of these, it is the **Least Common Multiple** (LCM) of 6 and 9.

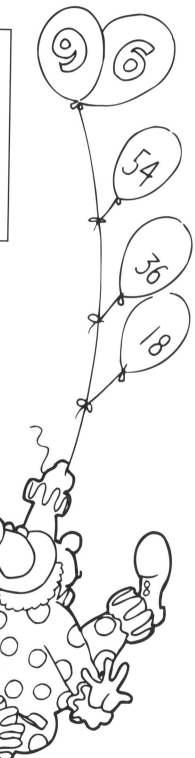

1. Write the first 8 multiples of 3, 4, and 6.

3, _____, _____, _____, _____, _____, _____, _____

4, _____, _____, _____, _____, _____, _____, _____

6, _____, _____, _____, _____, _____, _____, _____

2. What are the common multiples of 3, 4, and 6?

_____ and _____

3. What is the LCM of 3, 4, and 6? _____

4. What is the LCM for each of the following sets of numbers?

a. 5 and 3 _____   **d.** 3, 6, and 8 _____

b. 7 and 2 _____   **e.** 4, 5, and 10 _____

c. 6 and 9 _____   **f.** 4, 6, and 9 _____

Positively Prime

A **prime number's** only factors are 1 and itself.

1. Can an even number be prime? Explain.

2. Are all odd numbers prime? Explain.

3. Is the product of 2 prime numbers also prime? Explain.

4. Look at a multiplication table. What can you say about the numbers inside the table?

5. Consider the number 143.

    a. Is 2 a factor? _____

    b. Is 3, 6, or 9 a factor? _____

    c. Is 4 or 8 a factor? _____

    d. Is 5 or 10 a factor? _____

    e. Is 7 a factor? _____

    f. Do you think 143 is prime? _____

    g. Try dividing 143 by prime numbers larger than 10. Can you find a factor?

    h. Is 143 prime?

6. Find all the prime numbers between 2 and 100.

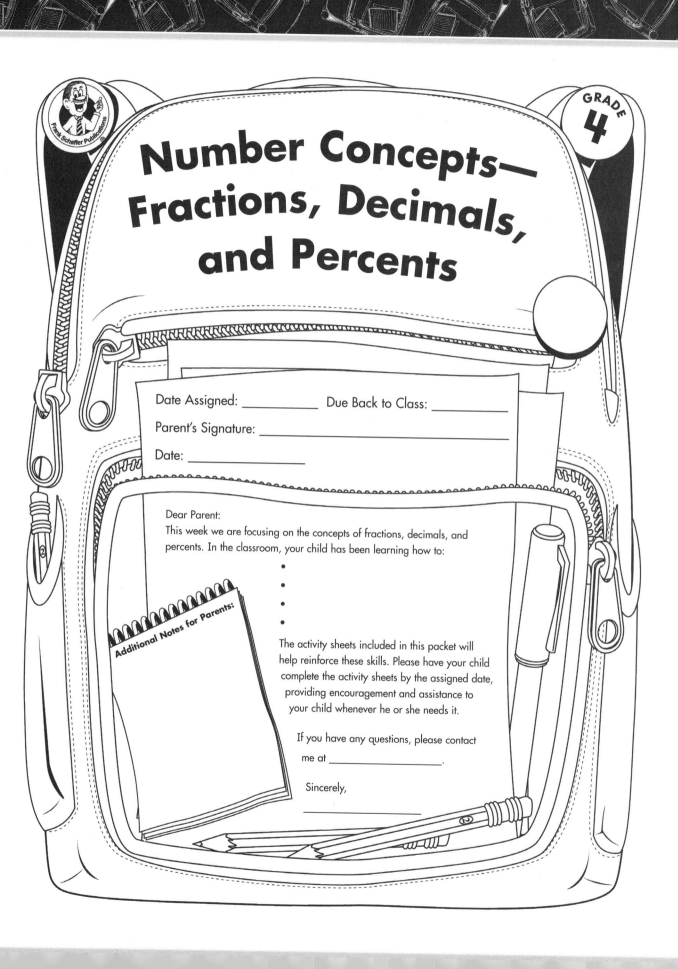

GRADE
4

Number Concepts—
Fractions, Decimals,
and Percents

Date Assigned: _____ Due Back to Class: _____

Parent's Signature: _____

Date: _____

Additional Notes for Parents:

Dear Parent:

This week we are focusing on the concepts of fractions, decimals, and percents. In the classroom, your child has been learning how to:

- •
- •
- •
- •

The activity sheets included in this packet will help reinforce these skills. Please have your child complete the activity sheets by the assigned date, providing encouragement and assistance to your child whenever he or she needs it.

If you have any questions, please contact me at _____.

Sincerely,

_____

To the Drawing Board

Draw each fraction two ways—as part of a whole and as part of a group.

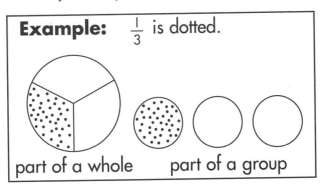

Example: $\frac{1}{3}$ is dotted.

part of a whole   part of a group

1. $\frac{2}{6}$ is red.

2. $\frac{1}{4}$ is dotted.

3. $\frac{2}{6}$ is striped.

4. $\frac{3}{3}$ is yellow.

5. $\frac{1}{2}$ is blue.

6. $\frac{7}{9}$ is starred.

7. $\frac{4}{5}$ is shaded.

8. $\frac{5}{8}$ is dotted.

9. $\frac{2}{2}$ is white.

Power Practice

Make your own figure. Divide it into equal fractional parts. Describe it using fractions.

Fractions on the Number Line

Place each fraction on the number line. Make the mark and label it with the given fraction.

Example: Divide into fourths. Label these fractions: $\frac{3}{4}, \frac{2}{8}, \frac{4}{4}, \frac{1}{2}$.

0          $\frac{2}{8}$ $\frac{1}{2}$ $\frac{3}{4}$ $\frac{4}{4}$ (1)

1. Divide into sixths. Label these fractions: $\frac{1}{3}, \frac{4}{6}, \frac{1}{2}, \frac{5}{6}, \frac{1}{6}$.

0

2. Divide into fourths. Label these fractions: $\frac{1}{2}, \frac{3}{4}, \frac{1}{4}, \frac{2}{4}$.

0

3. Divide into tenths. Label these fractions: $\frac{7}{10}, \frac{1}{2}, \frac{3}{5}, \frac{2}{10}, \frac{8}{10}$.

0

4. Divide into eighths. Label these fractions: $\frac{5}{8}, \frac{3}{4}, \frac{7}{8}, \frac{2}{4}, \frac{2}{8}$.

0

5. Divide into tenths. Label these fractions: $\frac{1}{5}, \frac{3}{10}, \frac{9}{10}, \frac{4}{5}, \frac{2}{5}$.

0

6. Divide into sixths. Label these fractions: $\frac{2}{6}, \frac{2}{3}, \frac{3}{6}, \frac{3}{3}, \frac{5}{6}$.

0

Name _____

Greater Than, Less Than, or Equal?

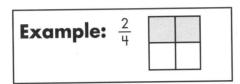

Example: $\frac{2}{4}$

1. Sketch and shade each fraction in the box above it.

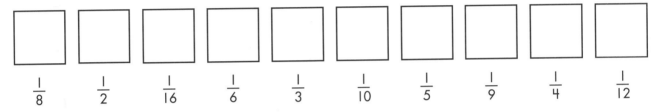

$\frac{1}{8}$ $\frac{1}{2}$ $\frac{1}{16}$ $\frac{1}{6}$ $\frac{1}{3}$ $\frac{1}{10}$ $\frac{1}{5}$ $\frac{1}{9}$ $\frac{1}{4}$ $\frac{1}{12}$

2. Place the above fractions on the number line.

<-----|--------------------------------|----->
    0   1

3. Use the sketches and number line to compare the fractions. Write >, <, or =
between the fractions.

a. $\frac{1}{16}$ ____ $\frac{1}{12}$ **b.** $\frac{1}{2}$ ____ $\frac{1}{6}$ **c.** $\frac{1}{3}$ ____ $\frac{1}{3}$

d. $\frac{1}{5}$ ____ $\frac{1}{8}$ **e.** $\frac{1}{12}$ ____ $\frac{1}{4}$ **f.** $\frac{1}{4}$ ____ $\frac{1}{2}$

g. $\frac{1}{2}$ ____ $\frac{1}{10}$ **h.** $\frac{1}{16}$ ____ $\frac{1}{9}$ **i.** $\frac{1}{3}$ ____ $\frac{1}{8}$

Name _____

The Same Size Piece

Fill in the boxes to make equivalent fractions.

1. $\dfrac{2}{4} = \dfrac{\boxed{}}{8}$

2. $\dfrac{3}{9} = \dfrac{1}{\boxed{}}$

3. $\dfrac{\boxed{}}{12} = \dfrac{4}{6}$

4. $\dfrac{1}{4} = \dfrac{\boxed{}}{12}$

5. $\dfrac{8}{\boxed{}} = \dfrac{2}{4}$

6. $\dfrac{2}{3} = \dfrac{4}{\boxed{}}$

7. $\dfrac{1}{2} = \dfrac{\boxed{}}{8}$

8. $\dfrac{\boxed{}}{16} = \dfrac{3}{4}$

9. $\dfrac{2}{3} = \dfrac{14}{\boxed{}}$

Evaluate the given fractions. Do the students have units that are equivalent in size? Explain. Prove your answer with a sketch or with an example of an equivalent fraction.

10. Arra has $\dfrac{2}{3}$ of a candy bar. Brenda has $\dfrac{5}{6}$ of a candy bar.

11. Choka drank $\dfrac{4}{8}$ of a carton of milk. Dylan drank $\dfrac{5}{10}$ of a carton of milk.

12. Ernie practiced his horn for $\dfrac{3}{4}$ of an hour. Fiona practiced her horn for $\dfrac{16}{20}$ of an hour.

13. Gabriella used $\dfrac{3}{8}$ of a yard of string. Joseph used $\dfrac{3}{4}$ of a yard of string.

14. Irene ate $\dfrac{12}{16}$ of her pizza. Jennifer ate $\dfrac{9}{12}$ of her pizza.

Fractions in Lowest Terms

| $\dfrac{6}{20}$ | Find the largest number that will divide evenly into both. Divide both the numerator and the denominator by that amount. $$\dfrac{6}{20} \div \dfrac{2}{2} = \dfrac{3}{10}$$ | $\dfrac{6}{20} = \dfrac{3}{10}$ |

Reduce the following fractions to lowest terms.

1. $\dfrac{5}{20} =$

2. $\dfrac{8}{20} =$

3. $\dfrac{3}{15} =$

4. $\dfrac{12}{20} =$

5. $\dfrac{2}{8} =$

6. $\dfrac{12}{16} =$

7. $\dfrac{14}{16} =$

8. $\dfrac{4}{8} =$

9. $\dfrac{9}{12} =$

10. $\dfrac{5}{10} =$

11. $\dfrac{6}{10} =$

12. $\dfrac{10}{15} =$

13. $\dfrac{2}{4} =$

14. $\dfrac{4}{8} =$

15. $\dfrac{6}{24} =$

16. $\dfrac{6}{8} =$

17. $\dfrac{8}{16} =$

18. $\dfrac{2}{12} =$

Name _____

Hundredths

Write the decimal that is equal to each word phrase on the first line. Write the equivalent fraction or mixed fraction on the second line.

1. four hundredths _____ _____

2. eight hundredths _____ _____

3. six hundredths _____ _____

4. thirteen hundredths _____ _____

5. nineteen hundredths _____ _____

6. forty-one hundredths _____ _____

7. eighty-nine hundredths

   _____ _____

8. five and three hundredths

   _____ _____

9. six and one hundredth

   _____ _____

10. twenty-seven and seventy-two hundredths _____ _____

11. three thousand, five hundred forty-two and six hundredths

    _____ _____

12. nine hundred and five hundredths

    _____ _____

13. two thousand, seven hundred one and two hundredths

    _____ _____

14. three hundred sixty-five and eleven hundredths _____ _____

If the grid is worth one, shade the following decimals.

15. 0.05

16. 0.03

17. 0.18

18. 0.54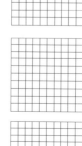

19. 0.87

20. 0.29

Match Them Up

Draw a line to match the word to its correct numeral fraction. Write the decimal that is equal to it on the line.

1. forty hundredths

2. six tenths

3. four and fifty-nine hundredths

4. six thousand and eleven hundredths

5. five and two tenths

6. ninety-eight hundredths

7. eight and four hundredths

8. seventy and one tenth

9. nine hundred one and twenty-two hundredths

10. fifty-four hundredths

11. forty-nine and three tenths

12. one thousand ten and four hundredths

a. $6{,}000 \frac{11}{100}$ _____

b. $70 \frac{1}{10}$ _____

c. $8 \frac{4}{100}$ _____

d. $49 \frac{3}{10}$ _____

e. $\frac{40}{100}$ _____

f. $1{,}010 \frac{4}{100}$ _____

g. $4 \frac{59}{100}$ _____

h. $901 \frac{22}{100}$ _____

i. $5 \frac{2}{10}$ _____

j. $\frac{6}{10}$ _____

k. $\frac{54}{100}$ _____

l. $\frac{98}{100}$ _____

Decimal Rounding

Round each number to the nearest tenth.

1. 5.2369 _____   **3.** 0.96 _____   **5.** 29.95 _____

2. 18.364 _____   **4.** 148.213 _____   **6.** 5.127 _____

Round each number to the nearest hundredth.

7. 0.234 _____   **9.** 29.065 _____   **11.** 967.497 _____

8. 63.482 _____   **10.** 0.0834 _____   **12.** 6.3811 _____

Round each number to the nearest thousandth.

13. 0.006341 _____   **15.** 3.4012 _____   **17.** 541.7302 _____

14. 0.26527 _____   **16.** 63.0427 _____   **18.** 700.9276 _____

Pleading the Fifth

A **percent** tells how many out of 100 equal parts.

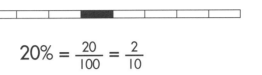

$$20\% = \frac{20}{100} = \frac{2}{10}$$

1. Look at the bar.

    a. What fraction of the bar is shaded? _____

    b. Draw lines to divide the bar into tenths. Write the fraction in tenths. _____

    c. How many hundredths would this be? _____

    d. What percentage of the bar is shaded? _____

2. What percentage is equal to $\frac{2}{5}$?

$\frac{2}{5} = \frac{1}{5} +$ _____ $=$ _____% + _____% = _____%

3. What percentage is equal to $\frac{3}{5}$? $\frac{4}{5}$? Show your work.

Power Practice

The fraction $\frac{1}{3}$ is approximately 33%.
What percentage would be equal to $\frac{2}{3}$? Explain.

What Part of the Whole?

Solve the following problems. Use sketches to verify your answers.

1. Ten students played on the soccer team. Four of the players kicked in a point.
    a. What fraction of the players kicked a goal? _____
    b. Write as a decimal. _____
    c. Write as a percent. _____

2. Jacob purchased ten pencils. Seven of the pencils were yellow, the rest were blue.
    a. What percent of the pencils were blue? _____
    b. Write as a decimal. _____
    c. Write as a fraction. _____

3. Ten fish are in a fish tank. Four of them are goldfish.
    a. What fraction of the fish are not goldfish? _____
    b. Write as a percent. _____
    c. Write as a decimal. _____

4. Natalie sewed together one hundred squares. Forty-five of the squares are primary colors.
    a. What fraction of the squares are primary colored? _____
    b. Write as a decimal. _____
    c. Write as a percent. _____

5. One hundred chocolate bars were sold by room 27. On the first day, fifty-nine were sold. On the second day, the rest were sold.
    a. What fraction of the total were sold on the second day? _____
    b. Write as a decimal. _____
    c. Write as a percent. _____

6. One hundred coins are in a bank: 47% are pennies, 6% are quarters, 18% are dimes, and the rest are nickels.
    a. What percent of the coins are nickels? _____
    b. Write the fraction for the quarters. _____
    c. Write the decimal for the pennies. _____
    d. Write the fraction and decimal for the dimes. _____

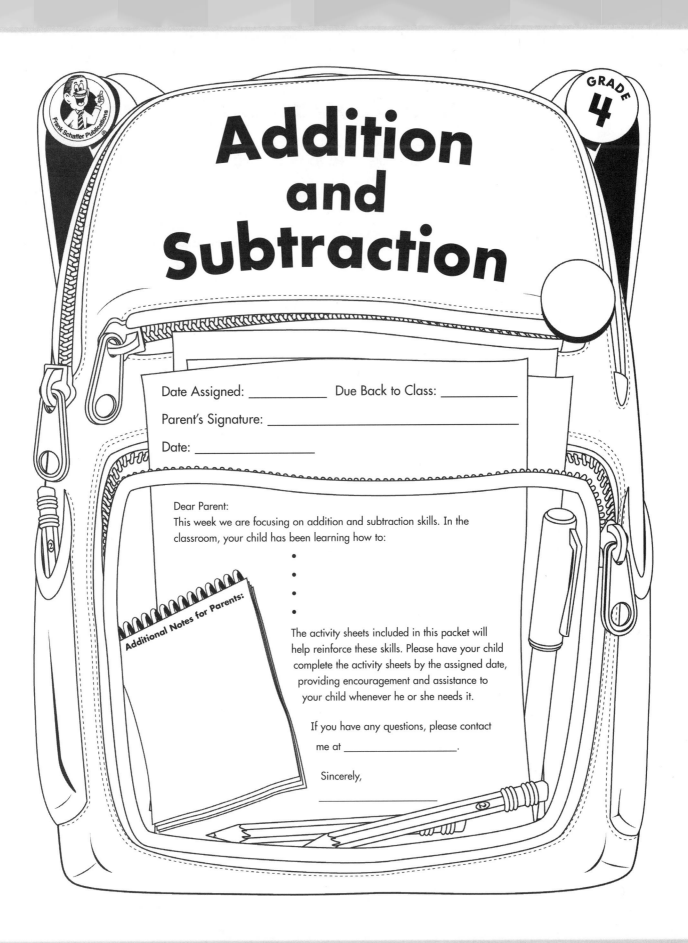

Addition and Subtraction

GRADE 4

Date Assigned: _____ Due Back to Class: _____

Parent's Signature: _____

Date: _____

Additional Notes for Parents:

Dear Parent:

This week we are focusing on addition and subtraction skills. In the classroom, your child has been learning how to:

- •
- •
- •

The activity sheets included in this packet will help reinforce these skills. Please have your child complete the activity sheets by the assigned date, providing encouragement and assistance to your child whenever he or she needs it.

If you have any questions, please contact me at _____.

Sincerely,

_____

Addition and Subtraction Families

The three numbers 4, 5, and 9 can be used to write two addition and two subtraction sentences:

4 + 5 = 9, 5 + 4 = 9
9 − 4 = 5, 9 − 5 = 4

This set of related number sentences is called a **fact family**.

Place the three numbers in the corners of the triangle. Put an asterisk by the largest number. Use the three numbers to write the four number sentences that make the fact family.

1. 7, 8, 15

____ + ____ = ____
____ + ____ = ____
____ − ____ = ____
____ − ____ = ____

2. 567, 321, 246

____ + ____ = ____
____ + ____ = ____
____ − ____ = ____
____ − ____ = ____

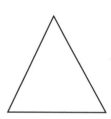

Find the number missing in the triangle. Use the three numbers to write the four number sentences that make the fact family.

3.

____ + ____ = ____
____ + ____ = ____
____ − ____ = ____
____ − ____ = ____

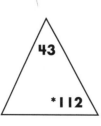

4.

____ + ____ = ____
____ + ____ = ____
____ − ____ = ____
____ − ____ = ____

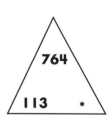

Adjust the Space

Subtraction looks for the space between two numbers.

If two numbers are adjusted equally, the answer to the problem stays the same.

The subtrahend, 57, is 3 away from 60; add 3 to both the **subtrahend** and the **minuend**.

minuend	71	+3	74
subtrahend	− 57	+3	− 60
	14		14

Look at the problem. Make an adjustment. Rewrite the problem and subtract.

1. 51
     − 26

2. 73
     − 49

3. 92
     − 48

4. 65
     − 17

5. 84
     − 56

6. 90
     − 24

7. 43
     − 37

8. 462
     − 428

9. 353
     − 327

10. 450
      − 280

Rebuilding the Pyramid

Add adjacent numbers together. Write their sum in the block above them. Continue adding until you reach the top block. Use your skills to fill in the missing blocks. Hint: Remember the relationship between addition and subtracting.

1.

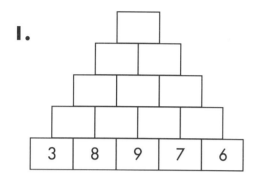

2.

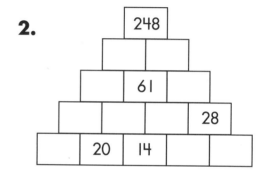

3.

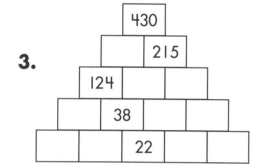

4.

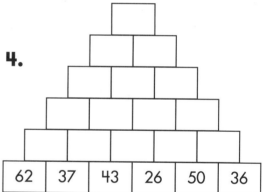

5.

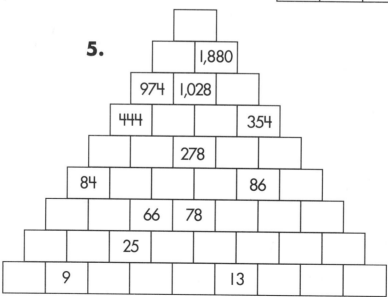

Name _____

Check With the Opposite

Solve. Check answers by using the opposite or **inverse operation**.

1. 9,214
      − 3,364

2. 5,329
      − 1,559

3. 2,783
      + 3,458

4. 4,827
      + 3,649

Solve and label. Check answers by using the opposite operation.

5. The used book sale had a total of 1,402 books. If 896 books were sold, how many are left?

6. Morgan has 345 trading cards in one stack, 648 trading cards in a second stack. How many cards does she have in all?

7. The ticket sales for the October home football game showed 1,257 spectators attended from the visiting teams and 4,071 spectators attended from the home team. How many more home team spectators bought tickets?

8. Ian has $45.78 in his bank account. The bike he wants to buy is $102.34. How much additional money does he need to purchase the bike?

Name _____

Using Estimation

Round each problem to the first digit. Find the estimated answer using your rounded numbers. Solve the original problem. Compare the actual and estimated answers.

	actual	**estimate**		**actual**	**estimate**
1.	457 + 824	+ _____	**7.**	6,793 + 3,382	+ _____
2.	566 + 783	+ _____	**8.**	8,520 – 1,704	– _____
3.	872 – 495	– _____	**9.**	7,723 – 4,376	– _____
4.	901 – 554	– _____	**10.**	5,562 + 2,679	+ _____
5.	658 + 272	+ _____	**11.**	6,342 – 5,463	– _____
6.	513 – 156	– _____	**12.**	7,456 – 3,748	– _____

Power Practice

Round the answers of the original problems. How do you explain estimated answers that are not equal to the rounded answers?

Paying the Bills

Add and subtract to find the total for each bill. If you have a credit, deduct it from your total bill. Then, write a check to pay each bill.

1. Utilities

Water:	$78.50
Gas:	$24.55
Electricity:	$65.44
Total =	_____

2. Waste

Trash:	$22.65
Recycling:	$10.00
Total =	_____

3. Phone

Local:	$15.00
Long Distance:	$22.95
Credit:	+$5.00
Total =	_____

4. Television

Regular:	$15.50
Movie Channels:	$12.75
Credit:	+$3.50
Total =	_____

Check 1:
```
                                    74-5/743
                                    0204682957        #_____
_____
                              Date_____
_____
PAY TO THE
ORDER OF_____   $_____
_____DOLLARS
SCHOOL BANK
777 LEARNING WAY
Memo_____   _____ MP
I:074300025I:0204682957II"0681
```

Check 2:
```
                                    74-5/743
                                    0204682957        #_____
_____
                              Date_____
_____
PAY TO THE
ORDER OF_____   $_____
_____DOLLARS
SCHOOL BANK
777 LEARNING WAY
Memo_____   _____ MP
I:074300025I:0204682957II"0681
```

Check 3:
```
                                    74-5/743
                                    0204682957        #_____
_____
                              Date_____
_____
PAY TO THE
ORDER OF_____   $_____
_____DOLLARS
SCHOOL BANK
777 LEARNING WAY
Memo_____   _____ MP
I:074300025I:0204682957II"0681
```

Check 4:
```
                                    74-5/743
                                    0204682957        #_____
_____
                              Date_____
_____
PAY TO THE
ORDER OF_____   $_____
_____DOLLARS
SCHOOL BANK
777 LEARNING WAY
Memo_____   _____ MP
I:074300025I:0204682957II"0681
```

Name _____

Decimals

When you add or subtract decimals, remember to include the decimal in your answer.

1. 4.2
$+ 5.2$

2. 6.4
$+ 1.4$

3. 3.1
$+ 7.8$

4. 4.7
$+ 3.2$

5. 4.9
$+ 2.0$

6. 5.9
$- 3.2$

7. 6.7
$- 5.6$

8. 7.8
$- 2.5$

9. 5.8
$- 3.3$

10. 3.9
$- 1.5$

11. $.23$
$+ .25$

12. $.43$
$+ .16$

13. $.26$
$+ .42$

14. $.64$
$+ .15$

15. $.68$
$+ .31$

Name _____

Here Come Decimals

Solve. Use the inverse operation to check your answer.

1. 156.82
    + 24.65

4.   89.201
    − 34.031

7. 701.5
    − 34.62

10. 124.63
     − 87.441

2.   45.663
    + 1.98

5. 421.93
    − 22.64

8.   94.61
    − 43.452

11.   6.02
     − 0.345

3. 365.1
    + 36.55

6.   12.97
    + 8.56

9.   8.746
    + 5.367

12.   54.782
     + 43.446

13. Use the answers to problems 1 through 12. Shade any sections in the circle that match an answer.

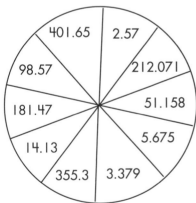

401.65 2.57 212.071 51.158 5.675 3.379 355.3 14.13 181.47 98.57

14. Look at the shaded part of the answer circle.

    a. Write the fraction. _____

    b. Write the decimal. _____

    c. Write the percent. _____

    d. Write the word form of the fraction. _____

All Together Now

Shade the parts to find the sum of each set of fractions.

1. ○○○○○○ $\frac{1}{6} + \frac{4}{6} =$ _____

2. ○○○○ $\frac{1}{4} + \frac{1}{4} =$ _____

3. ○○○○○○○○○○ $\frac{4}{10} + \frac{3}{10} =$ _____

4. ○○○○○○○ $\frac{3}{7} + \frac{2}{7} =$ _____

5. ○○○○○○○○ $\frac{2}{9} + \frac{1}{9} =$ _____

6. ○○○○○ $\frac{1}{5} + \frac{3}{5} =$ _____

7. ○○○○○○○○ $\frac{4}{8} + \frac{2}{8} =$ _____

8. ○○○ $\frac{1}{3} + \frac{2}{3} =$ _____

Find the sum of each set of fractions. Use sketches if needed.

9. $\frac{2}{4} + \frac{1}{4} =$ _____

10. $\frac{5}{9} + \frac{2}{9} =$ _____

11. $\frac{7}{12} + \frac{3}{12} =$ _____

12. $\frac{3}{6} + \frac{1}{6} =$ _____

13. $\frac{1}{8} + \frac{1}{8} =$ _____

14. $\frac{6}{11} + \frac{3}{11} =$ _____

Tossing Some Out

Find the difference by crossing out shaded boxes.

1. $\frac{2}{3} - \frac{1}{3} =$ _____

2. $\frac{6}{8} - \frac{3}{8} =$ _____

3. $\frac{3}{5} - \frac{1}{5} =$ _____

4. $\frac{7}{10} - \frac{3}{10} =$ _____

5. $\frac{4}{6} - \frac{1}{6} =$ _____

6. $\frac{4}{4} - \frac{1}{4} =$ _____

7. $\frac{9}{12} - \frac{5}{12} =$ _____

8. $\frac{6}{7} - \frac{2}{7} =$ _____

Find the difference of each set of fractions. Make a sketch if you need it.

9. $\frac{5}{8} - \frac{1}{8} =$ _____

10. $\frac{6}{9} - \frac{2}{9} =$ _____

11. $\frac{8}{12} - \frac{3}{12} =$ _____

12. $\frac{3}{4} - \frac{2}{4} =$ _____

13. $\frac{5}{10} - \frac{3}{10} =$ _____

14. $\frac{2}{2} - \frac{1}{2} =$ _____

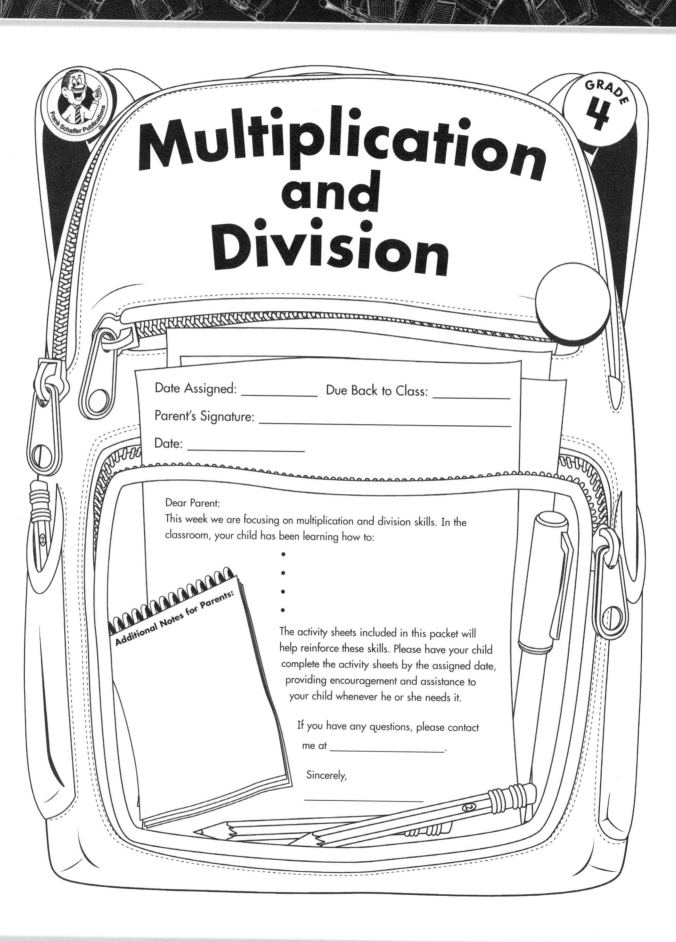

Multiplication and Division

GRADE 4

Date Assigned: _____ Due Back to Class: _____

Parent's Signature: _____

Date: _____

Additional Notes for Parents:

Dear Parent:

This week we are focusing on multiplication and division skills. In the classroom, your child has been learning how to:

•
•
•
•

The activity sheets included in this packet will help reinforce these skills. Please have your child complete the activity sheets by the assigned date, providing encouragement and assistance to your child whenever he or she needs it.

If you have any questions, please contact me at _____.

Sincerely,

_____

Name _____

Commutative and Associative Properties

The **commutative property** says you can switch the order of the numbers and still get the same answer.	The **associative property** says you can change the grouping of the numbers and still get the same answer.
$5 + 10 = 10 + 5$ $5 \times 2 = 2 \times 5$ $15 = 15$ $10 = 10$	$(3 + 5) + 6 = 3 + (5 + 6)$ $(3 \times 5) \times 6 = 3 \times (5 \times 6)$ $8 + 6 = 3 + 11$ $15 \times 6 = 3 \times 30$ $14 = 14$ $90 = 90$

Identify the property that makes each of these number sentences true. Write A for the associative property or C for the commutative property.

_____ **1.** $59 + 43 = 43 + 59$

_____ **2.** $(7 + 8) + 6 = 7 + (8 + 6)$

_____ **3.** $(5 + 2) + 3 = 3 + (5 + 2)$

_____ **4.** $5 \times (8 \times 6) = (5 \times 8) \times 6$

_____ **5.** $3 \times 2 = 2 \times 3$

_____ **6.** $412 \times (13 \times 15) = 412 \times (15 \times 13)$

Rewrite each of the expressions in an equivalent form, using the property indicated.

7. $4 \times 3 =$ _____ commutative

8. $5 + 8 + 6 =$ _____ commutative

9. $7 \times (4 \times 3) =$ _____ associative

10. $7 \times (4 \times 3) =$ _____ commutative

11. $(8 + 4) + 2 =$ _____ associative

12. $2 \times (3 \times 6) \times 4 =$ _____ associative

Division

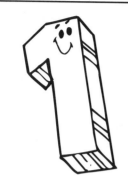

Mr. 1 Rules

1. Any number divided by 1 is that number.

2. Any number (not zero) divided by itself is 1.

$$1\overline{)4} = 4 \qquad 4\overline{)4} = 1$$

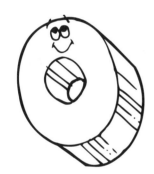

Mr. 0 Rules

3. Zero divided by any number is zero.

4. Never divide by zero.

$$6\overline{)0} = 0 \qquad 0\overline{)7} \text{ not possible}$$

Divide to find the answers. Write which rule is being expressed.

1. $1\overline{)8}$ Rule _____

2. $4 \div 1$ Rule _____

3. $5\overline{)0}$ Rule _____

4. $9 \div 0$ Rule _____

5. $3\overline{)3}$ Rule _____

6. $0 \div 2$ Rule _____

7. $0\overline{)2}$ Rule _____

8. $6 \div 6$ Rule _____

Distributive Property

The **distributive property** is used when there is a combination of multiplication over addition or subtraction.

$$5(3 + 6) = 5 \times 3 + 5 \times 6$$
$$5 \times 9 = 15 + 30$$
$$45 = 45$$

$$16 - 6 = (8 \times 2) - (3 \times 2)$$
$$10 = (8 - 3)2$$
$$10 = 10$$

Use the distributive property to rewrite the following expressions. Then, use the correct order of operations to solve both sides and check your answers.

1. $2(6 + 3) =$

2. $12 + 9 =$

3. $4(9 - 1) =$

4. $18 - 6 =$

5. $(15 - 3)2 =$

6. $(7 + 5)8 =$

7. $25 - 15 =$

8. $3(5 + 6) =$

9. $8 + 12 =$

Multiplication and Division Families

The three numbers 4, 3, and 12 can be used to write two multiplication and two division sentences:

$$4 \times 3 = 12, \quad 3 \times 4 = 12$$
$$12 \div 3 = 4, \quad 12 \div 4 = 3$$

This set of related number sentences is called a **fact family**.

Place the three numbers in the corners of the triangle. Put an asterisk by the largest number. Use the three numbers to write the four number sentences that make the fact family.

1. 8, 7, 56

_____ x _____ = _____
_____ x _____ = _____
_____ ÷ _____ = _____
_____ ÷ _____ = _____

2. 24, 192, 8

_____ x _____ = _____
_____ x _____ = _____
_____ ÷ _____ = _____
_____ ÷ _____ = _____

Find the number missing in the triangle. Use the three numbers to write the four number sentences that make the fact family.

3.

_____ x _____ = _____
_____ x _____ = _____
_____ ÷ _____ = _____
_____ ÷ _____ = _____

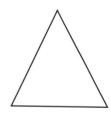

4.

_____ x _____ = _____
_____ x _____ = _____
_____ ÷ _____ = _____
_____ ÷ _____ = _____

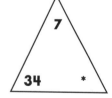

Power Practice

Choose one fact family. Draw the triangle and list the four number sentences of the family on the back of this page.

Name _____

Groups

Multiplication requires counting groups with an equal number of objects in each set. Multiplication is also a form of repeated addition.

15 + 15 + 15 + 15 = 60

$$
\begin{array}{r}
15 \\
\times\ \ 4 \\
\hline
60
\end{array}
$$

— number of objects in each set is the **factor**
— number of groups or sets is the **factor**
— total number of objects is the **product**

Make a sketch for each multiplication problem. Write the repeated addition problem beside the sets. Find the product.

1.
$$
\begin{array}{r}
33 \\
\times\ \ 4 \\
\hline
\end{array}
$$

2.
$$
\begin{array}{r}
25 \\
\times\ \ 8 \\
\hline
\end{array}
$$

3.
$$
\begin{array}{r}
56 \\
\times\ \ 2 \\
\hline
\end{array}
$$

4.
$$
\begin{array}{r}
49 \\
\times\ \ 3 \\
\hline
\end{array}
$$

5.
$$
\begin{array}{r}
41 \\
\times\ \ 6 \\
\hline
\end{array}
$$

6.
$$
\begin{array}{r}
253 \\
\times\ \ 2 \\
\hline
\end{array}
$$

7.
$$
\begin{array}{r}
138 \\
\times\ \ 3 \\
\hline
\end{array}
$$

8.
$$
\begin{array}{r}
785 \\
\times\ \ 1 \\
\hline
\end{array}
$$

MATH

·LOST & FOUND·

FACTORS

Multiplication

$$
\begin{array}{r} 65 \\ \times\ 24 \\ \hline \end{array}
\qquad
\begin{array}{r} {}^{2}65 \\ \times\ 24 \\ \hline 260 \end{array}
\qquad
\begin{array}{r} {}^{1}\ {}^{2}65 \\ \times\ 24 \\ \hline 260 \\ 130\ \ \end{array}
\qquad
\begin{array}{r} {}^{1}\ {}^{2}65 \\ \times\ 24 \\ \hline 260 \\ 130\ \ \\ \hline 1{,}560 \end{array}
$$

Multiply to find the answers.

1.
$$\begin{array}{r} 11 \\ \times\ 54 \\ \hline \end{array}$$

2.
$$\begin{array}{r} 28 \\ \times\ 11 \\ \hline \end{array}$$

3.
$$\begin{array}{r} 65 \\ \times\ 22 \\ \hline \end{array}$$

4.
$$\begin{array}{r} 19 \\ \times\ 49 \\ \hline \end{array}$$

5.
$$\begin{array}{r} 98 \\ \times\ 12 \\ \hline \end{array}$$

6.
$$\begin{array}{r} 36 \\ \times\ 15 \\ \hline \end{array}$$

7.
$$\begin{array}{r} 42 \\ \times\ 25 \\ \hline \end{array}$$

8.
$$\begin{array}{r} 19 \\ \times\ 37 \\ \hline \end{array}$$

9.
$$\begin{array}{r} 49 \\ \times\ 38 \\ \hline \end{array}$$

10.
$$\begin{array}{r} 19 \\ \times\ 48 \\ \hline \end{array}$$

11.
$$\begin{array}{r} 56 \\ \times\ 61 \\ \hline \end{array}$$

12.
$$\begin{array}{r} 45 \\ \times\ 32 \\ \hline \end{array}$$

13.
$$\begin{array}{r} 37 \\ \times\ 84 \\ \hline \end{array}$$

14.
$$\begin{array}{r} 68 \\ \times\ 98 \\ \hline \end{array}$$

15.
$$\begin{array}{r} 28 \\ \times\ 85 \\ \hline \end{array}$$

Name _____

More Multiplication

Find the answers. Use the code to discover how the word *great* is spelled in each language.

Row 1					
Swahili	**1.** 367 x 88	**2.** 211 x 26	**3.** 744 x 75	**4.** 861 x 44	**5.** 524 x 38

Row 2					
Dutch	**6.** 682 x 95	**7.** 553 x 64	**8.** 724 x 49	**9.** 648 x 89	**10.** 472 x 84

Row 3					
Spanish	**11.** 351 x 65	**12.** 438 x 95	**13.** 942 x 72	**14.** 313 x 78	**15.** 946 x 48

5,486	= J	35,392	= O	45,408	= O
19,912	= U	35,476	= E	55,800	= A
22,815	= B	37,884	= B	57,672	= D
24,414	= N	39,648	= !	64,790	= G
32,296	= A	41,610	= U	67,824	= E

GREAT!
English

Numbers in the Groups

Division requires equal distribution of objects into sets. When filling the sets, objects can be placed in the sets one at a time or in groups. As long as an equal amount is placed in each group until the total is in the group, you will arrive at the same answer.

Example: Divide 18 items into 3 sets.

$18 \div 3$

Fill each set with 4 and then with 2. **or** Fill each set by 2's.

Draw the sets for each problem. Fill in the sets with the given number. Show two different ways to fill in the sets.

1. $28 \div 7 =$ _____

2. $36 \div 6 =$ _____

3. $36 \div 4 =$ _____

4. $56 \div 8 =$ _____

5. $49 \div 7 =$ _____

6. $64 \div 8 =$ _____

7. $72 \div 9 =$ _____

8. $42 \div 6 =$ _____

9. $14 \div 2 =$ _____

10. $15 \div 5 =$ _____

Divide and Conquer

Solve. Add the answers in each small box. In the large box, circle the correct sum of the answers for that group of problems. Use the inverse operation to check your answers.

1. $7\overline{)378}$ ☐

2. $9\overline{)612}$ ☐

3. $5\overline{)415}$ ☐

189, 211, 205, 221

4. $8\overline{)752}$ ☐

5. $4\overline{)232}$ ☐

6. $6\overline{)282}$ ☐

199, 201, 187, 204

7. $33\overline{)660}$ ☐

8. $6\overline{)438}$ ☐

9. $40\overline{)840}$ ☐

121, 107, 94, 114

Name _____

Compare the Prices

Look at each pair of items shown below. Circle the less expensive item for each problem. Explain your answer.

1.

12-ounce bottle of shampoo	24-ounce bottle of shampoo
$2.25	**$5.00**

2.

four 12 packs of soda	one 12 pack of soda
$10.00	**$1.99**

3.

16-ounce can of soup	10-ounce can of soup
$1.19	**$0.89**

4.

24-ounce bottle of water	12-ounce bottle of water
$1.25	**$0.75**

5.

one box of 3 soaps	one box of 12 soaps
$1.55	**$3.10**

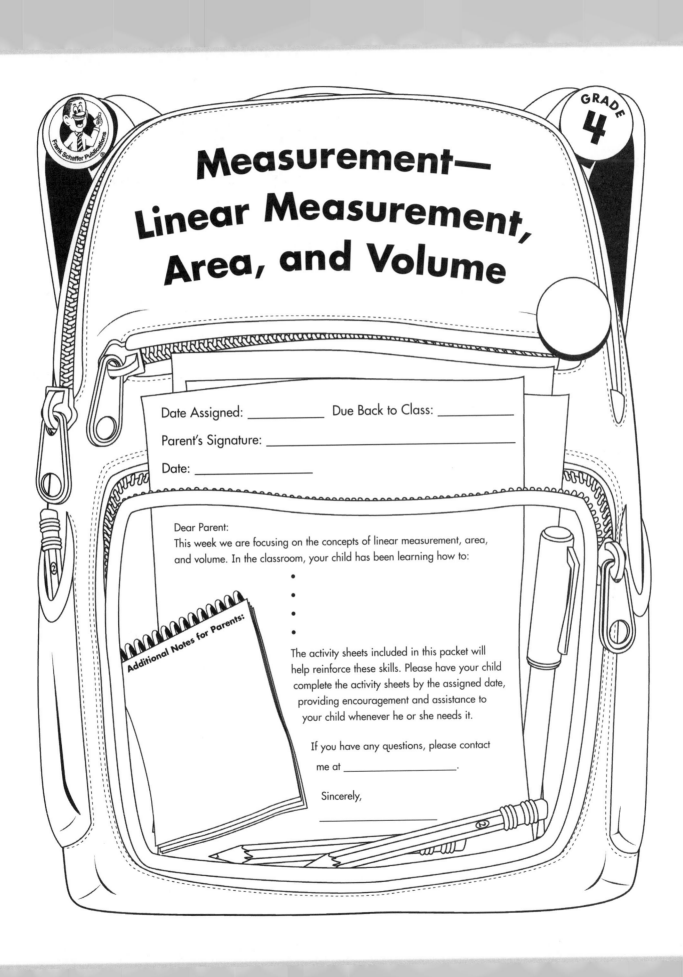

Measurement— Linear Measurement, Area, and Volume

GRADE 4

Date Assigned: _____ Due Back to Class: _____

Parent's Signature: _____

Date: _____

Additional Notes for Parents:

Dear Parent:

This week we are focusing on the concepts of linear measurement, area, and volume. In the classroom, your child has been learning how to:

- •
- •
- •
- •

The activity sheets included in this packet will help reinforce these skills. Please have your child complete the activity sheets by the assigned date, providing encouragement and assistance to your child whenever he or she needs it.

If you have any questions, please contact me at _____.

Sincerely,

_____

Customary Length Units

Fill in each answer blank with one of the following standard units of measurement: *inch*, *foot*, *yard*, or *mile*.

1. Marta runs three _____ in 30 minutes.

2. The length of Max's swimming pool is about 15 _____.

3. The basketball net is about 10 _____ from the ground.

4. Kerry's ruler is 12 _____ long.

5. The giraffe at the zoo is about 18 _____ tall.

6. It takes me about 50 minutes to walk to school since my school is about 2 _____ from my house.

7. A box of tissues is about 10 _____ long.

8. The cup I made during pottery class is about $4\frac{1}{2}$ _____ high.

9. The shelf at the top of my closet is about 8 _____ high.

10. My Uncle John is about 6 _____ tall.

Power Practice

Write two more fill-in-the-blank measurement problems like the ones above. Write one about distance and one about length.

Convert Customary Units

Convert to the equivalent customary units. Write your answers on the lines provided.

1. 6 feet = _____ inches

2. 12 feet = _____ yards

3. 4 miles = _____ feet

4. 6 yards = _____ feet

5. 48 inches = _____ feet

6. $2\frac{1}{2}$ feet = _____ inches

7. 18 yards = _____ feet

8. 3 miles = _____ feet

9. $25\frac{1}{2}$ feet = _____ yards

10. 18 inches = _____ feet

Solve the following word problems.

11. Marissa and her brother built a snowman that was about 42 inches high. About how many feet high was the snowman?

12. Maggie needs about 18 yards of ribbon. One hundred inches of ribbon are sold on rolls for $2.49. How many rolls of ribbon will Maggie need to buy? How much will it cost Maggie to purchase the ribbon that she needs?

Power Practice

Write your own word problem that requires customary unit conversion.

Converting mm to cm

Convert the following millimeter amounts to centimeters.
Remember, 10 millimeters (mm) equal 1 centimeter (cm).

1. 30 mm = _____ cm

2. 90 mm = _____ cm

3. 60 mm = _____ cm

4. 140 mm = _____ cm

5. 10 mm = _____ cm

6. 160 mm = _____ cm

7. 110 mm = _____ cm

8. 50 mm = _____ cm

9. 180 mm = _____ cm

10. 130 mm = _____ cm

11. 80 mm = _____ cm

12. 190 mm = _____ cm

13. 40 mm = _____ cm

14. 120 mm = _____ cm

15. 200 mm = _____ cm

16. Explain how to convert millimeters to centimeters. Talk about the steps you took for each one. Draw a picture if it helps you explain.

_____

_____

_____

_____

Finding Perimeter and Area

Find the **perimeter** of each room below. Include the correct units in your answer.

1.

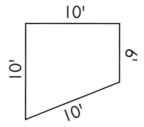

_____

2.

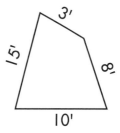

_____

3.

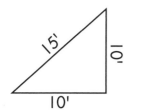

_____

Find the **area** of each room below. Include units in your answer.

4.

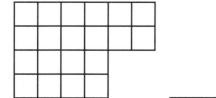

_____

5.

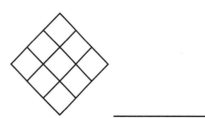

_____

6.

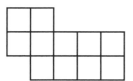

_____

Perimeter Word Problems

Solve these word problems.

1. Ingrid drew an octagon with chalk. The perimeter of the octagon is 960 inches. How long is each side?

2. The perimeter of a rectangular pool is 84 feet. The width of the pool is half the length. What are the measurements of the rectangular pool?

3. José is fencing in his square garden. The length of one side is 5 meters. How much fencing will José need to fence in his garden?

4. A square swimming pool has a perimeter of 64 meters. What is the length of each side of the square pool?

5. The triangular-shaped playground has a perimeter of 125 feet. One side is 62 feet and the second side is 48 feet. What is the length of the third side?

Power Practice

Write a story problem about perimeter. Use your school as the setting.

Area of Triangles, Rectangles, and Parallelograms

Area of a triangle = $\frac{1}{2}$ base x height	Area of a rectangle = length x width	Area of a parallelogram = base x height
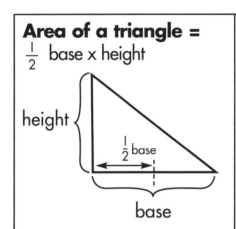	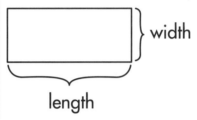	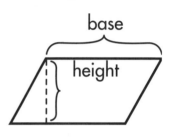

Determine the area of each figure.

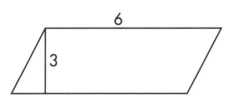

1. area _____

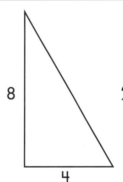

2. area _____

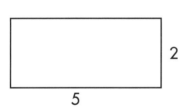

3. area _____

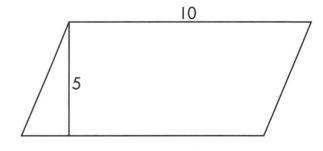

4. area _____

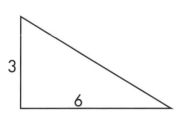

5. area _____

6. area _____

Using a Rule to Find Volume

One way to find **volume** is to use the following rule:

Volume = length x width x height

Use the formula to determine the volume of the figures below. Match each figure to its correct volume.

1.

height = ____   width = ____

length = ____

10 cubic units

2.

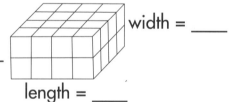

height = ____   width = ____

length = ____

6 cubic units

3.

height = ____   width = ____

length = ____

12 cubic units

4.

height = ____   width = ____

length = ____

18 cubic units

5.

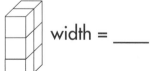

height = ____   width = ____

length = ____

32 cubic units

Name _____

Volume of Prisms

Write the volume of a rectangular prism with each of the following dimensions. Remember to label each volume in cubic units.

1. length = 6 units, width = 4 units, height = 2 units _____

2. length = 12 units, width = 8 units, height = 1 unit _____

3. length = $4\frac{1}{2}$ units, width = $4\frac{1}{2}$ units, height = 4 units _____

4. length = 10 units, width = 5 units, height = 5 units _____

5. length = $8\frac{1}{2}$ units, width = 12 units, height = 8 units _____

Look at each volume. Write the dimensions each prism could have.

6. 24 cubic units   length _____   width _____   height _____

7. 4 cubic units   length _____   width _____   height _____

8. 60 cubic units   length _____   width _____   height _____

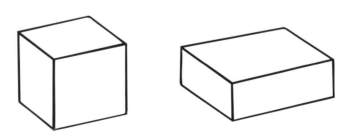

Power Practice

What formula do you use to find the volume of rectangular prisms? Would you use a different formula for different shapes?

Angle Names

Measure each angle with a protractor. Write *acute*, *obtuse*, or *right* on the line.

1.

_____
degrees

_____
name

2.

_____
degrees

_____
name

3.

_____
degrees

_____
name

4.

_____
degrees

_____
name

5.

_____
degrees

_____
name

6.

_____
degrees

_____
name

7.

_____
degrees

_____
name

8.

_____
degrees

_____
name

Angle Identification

Draw the following angles. Write the word *obtuse*, *acute*, or *right* for each problem to identify the type of angle.

1. Draw a 100° angle.

_____

2. Draw a 45° angle.

_____

3. Draw a 90° angle.

_____

4. Draw a 150° angle.

_____

5. Draw a 25° angle.

_____

6. Show times on the clocks below, using the hands to create the kinds of angles listed.

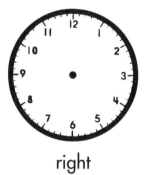
right

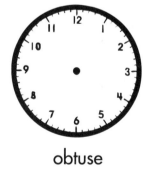
obtuse

acute

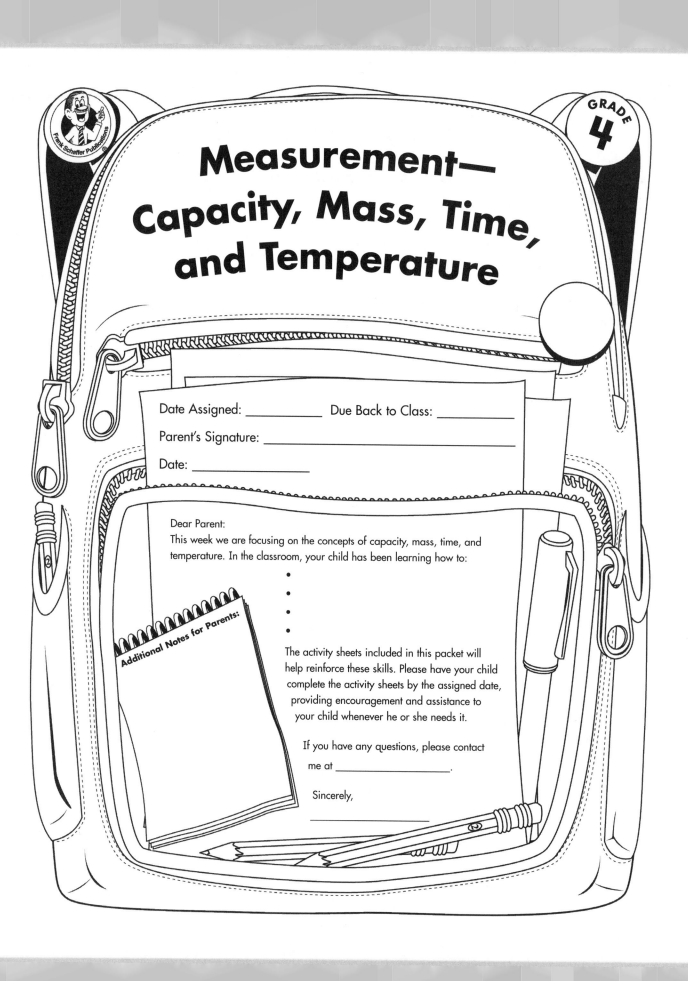

Measurement— Capacity, Mass, Time, and Temperature

GRADE 4

Date Assigned: _____ Due Back to Class: _____

Parent's Signature: _____

Date: _____

Dear Parent:

This week we are focusing on the concepts of capacity, mass, time, and temperature. In the classroom, your child has been learning how to:

- •
- •
- •
- •

The activity sheets included in this packet will help reinforce these skills. Please have your child complete the activity sheets by the assigned date, providing encouragement and assistance to your child whenever he or she needs it.

If you have any questions, please contact me at _____.

Sincerely,

_____

Additional Notes for Parents:

Converting Units of Measurement

The box below shows the customary units of capacity that are most often used in the kitchen. Use the box to complete the problems.

1. 4 quarts = _____ gallons

2. 5 cups = _____ fluid ounces

3. 3 cups = _____ tablespoons

4. 8 pints = _____ quarts

5. 16 fluid ounces = _____ cups

6. 10 quarts = _____ pints

7. 3 half gallons = _____ quarts

8. 1 gallon = _____ quarts

9. 8 quarts = _____ gallons

10. 18 teaspoons = _____ tablespoons

Key
1 tablespoon = 3 teaspoons
1 cup, dry = 16 tablespoons
1 cup, fluid = 8 fluid ounces
1 pint = 2 cups
1 quart = 2 pints
1 half gallon = 2 quarts
1 gallon = 4 quarts

Name _____

Recipe Measuring

Fruity Floats

1 gallon orange juice
2 quarts ginger ale
3 quarts vanilla ice cream
6 cups cran-apple juice

Blend all the ingredients together.

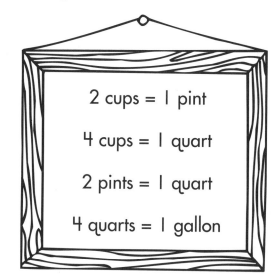

2 cups = 1 pint

4 cups = 1 quart

2 pints = 1 quart

4 quarts = 1 gallon

Read the recipe above. Answer the questions.

1. Is 1 quart of cran-apple juice enough for this recipe? _____

2. Are 8 cups of ginger ale enough for this recipe? _____

3. You have 2 quarts of cran-apple juice. How much will you have left over after making the recipe?

_____

4. Are 4 quarts of orange juice enough to make this recipe? _____

5. You have 3 pints of vanilla ice cream. Do you have enough to make this recipe?

_____

6. You have 1 gallon of ginger ale. How much will you have left over after making the recipe?

_____

Customary Weight

Fill in each answer with the unit that is appropriate. Choose the best unit: *ounce*, *pound*, or *ton*.

1. elephant _____

2. grown man _____

3. pen _____

4. large moving truck_____

5. cell phone _____

6. laptop computer_____

7. pair of shoelaces _____

8. pair of glasses _____

9. train_____

10. pair of running shoes _____

Power Practice

List one item that weighs each of the following weights: 1 pound, 5 pounds, 10 pounds, and 25 pounds.

Matching Weights

Match each measurement on the left to its equivalent on the right. Use the key to help you.

1. 4 lb.		**a.** 89 oz.	
2. 2 t.		**b.** 2 lb.	
3. 32 oz.		**c.** 143 oz.	
4. 6 t.		**d.** 12,000 lb.	
5. 3 lb.		**e.** 10,000 lb.	
6. 8 lb. 15 oz.		**f.** 112 oz.	
7. 5 t.		**g.** 4 lb.	
8. 5 lb. 9 oz.		**h.** 64 oz.	
9. 7 lb.		**i.** 48 oz.	
10. 64 oz.		**j.** 4,000 lb.	

Key

1 lb. = 16 oz.
1 t. = 2,000 lbs.

11. Choose two units from above. Explain the relationship between the two units. Write or draw to explain.

Metric Weight

Look at each object. Write *kilogram* or *gram* on the line, depending on the best unit of measurement for each item.

1. small roll of candy _____

2. bike _____

3. feather _____

4. thumbtack _____

5. stopwatch _____

6. television _____

7. large dog _____

8. person _____

9. Compare a gram and a kilogram using words.

_____

_____

_____

_____

Power Practice

Weigh yourself. Write your weight in grams. Write your weight in kilograms.

Time in Numbers and Words

Read each clock. Write each time in numbers and in words.

1.

_____

_____

2.

_____

_____

3.

_____

_____

4.

_____

_____

5.

_____

_____

6.

_____

_____

Power Practice

Add A.M. or P.M. to each time. Then, write one activity that you might be doing at each time

Time Word Problems

Use your knowledge of time to solve the problems.

1. The bell rings for recess to begin at 12:15 and rings again at 1:00 for recess to end. Tamika volunteers to help her teacher water the classroom plants for the first 10 minutes of recess. How many minutes will she have left to play kickball when she is finished? _____

2. Music class is every Thursday at 1:30. The students stay for 1 hour and 15 minutes. What time do they finish music class? _____

3. Principal Allen is making up the schedule for next year. The winter holiday will be two weeks instead of the usual ten days. Which is longer, 2 weeks or 10 days? _____

4. Room 6 will take a school trip to the museum on April 5. The teacher must call 48 hours before arriving to confirm the time of the tour. On what date must she call? _____

5. The trip to the museum takes 1 hour. If the students have traveled for 35 minutes on the bus, how many more minutes will it be until they arrive? _____

Name _____

Time Conversions

1 minute	=	60 seconds
1 hour	=	60 minutes
1 day	=	24 hours
1 week	=	7 days
1 month	=	28, 29, 30, or 31 days
1 year	=	365 days
		(366 during leap year)
1 decade	=	10 years

Match equivalent values.

1.	3 decades		48 hours
2.	1 year (not a leap year)		90 seconds
3.	3 minutes		14 days
4.	half a day		31 days
5.	2 weeks		40 years
6.	half-hour		12 hours
7.	a minute and a half		180 seconds
8.	2 days		30 years
9.	1 month		365 days
10.	4 decades		30 minutes

Name _____

Fahrenheit Temperature

What temperature is shown on each thermometer?

1. 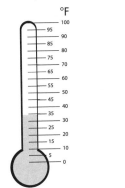 _____

2.  _____

3. 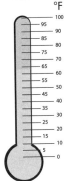 _____

4. 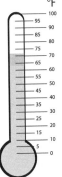 _____

Solve the following problems.

5. The temperature is 75°F. The temperature drops 10 degrees.
   What is the temperature now? _____

6. The temperature is 69°F. The temperature rises 3 degrees.
   What is the temperature now? _____

7. The temperature is 54°F. The temperature drops 12 degrees.
   What is the temperature now? _____

Power Practice

 How do you convert Fahrenheit temperatures to Celsius? Write directions in your own words.

Fill in the Thermometer

Fill in each thermometer with the temperature listed. Read each thermometer and write one sentence describing the temperature and one sentence describing the clothes you might choose to wear based on the temperature.

1. 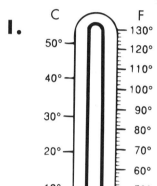 20 degrees Celsius _____

_____

_____

_____

2. 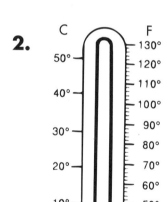 103 degrees Fahrenheit _____

_____

_____

_____

3. 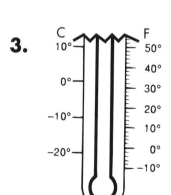 30 degrees Fahrenheit _____

_____

_____

_____

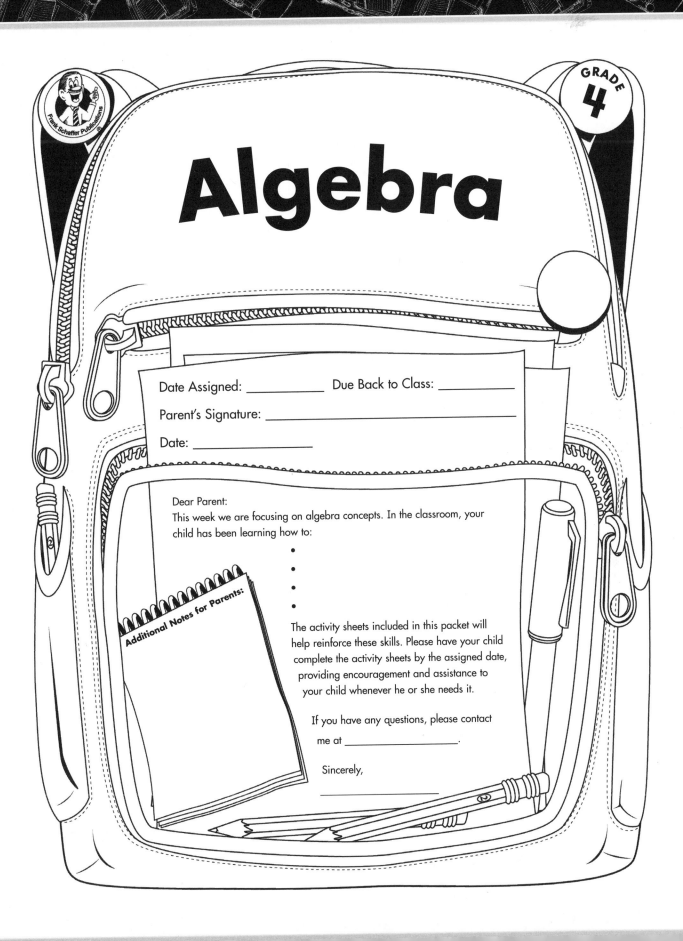

Algebra

GRADE 4

Date Assigned: _____ Due Back to Class: _____

Parent's Signature: _____

Date: _____

Additional Notes for Parents:

Dear Parent:

This week we are focusing on algebra concepts. In the classroom, your child has been learning how to:

- •
- •
- •
- •

The activity sheets included in this packet will help reinforce these skills. Please have your child complete the activity sheets by the assigned date, providing encouragement and assistance to your child whenever he or she needs it.

If you have any questions, please contact me at _____.

Sincerely,

_____

Pattern Match-Up

For each shape pattern, write the letter of the number pattern that matches it.

_____ 1.

_____ 2.

_____ 3.

_____ 4.

A. 0 1 0 1 0 1

B. 1 3 5 1 3 5

C. 3 5 5 3 5 5

D. 2 2 4 4 2 2

Name _____

The Case of the Missing Numbers

A **rule** describes the process used to create the pattern.

Example: 10 20 30 40 50   Rule: + 10

Find the patterns. Fill in the missing numbers in the pattern. Write the rule for each pattern.

1. 3 ____ ____ 18 23 28 ____ ____

Rule: _____

2. _____ 5,000,000 500,000 _____ 5,000 500 _____

Rule: _____

3. ____ 656 590 524 ____ ____ ____ 260

Rule: _____

4. 1.25 ____ ____ 80 320 1,280 _____ _____

Rule: _____

Power Practice

Prove that the numbers you chose and your rule work in the pattern. Start with the first number in the pattern. Use your rule to find the next number. Continue until you have found 8 numbers. Do these numbers match the ones you found in the problem?

Name _____

A Tidy Sum

For each pattern, find the amount of change between each pair of numbers. Then, answer the questions.

1. 4   5   9   14   23   37   60

    a. Is this a growing pattern or a decreasing pattern?

    b. Does this pattern change at a constant rate? How do you know?

    _____

    c. Describe how to find the next number in the pattern. _____

    d. Find the next 3 numbers in the pattern. _____ _____ _____

2. 267   165   102   63   39   24   15

    a. Is this a growing pattern or a decreasing pattern?

    b. Does this pattern change at a constant rate? How do you know?

    _____

    c. Describe how to find the next number in the pattern. _____

    d. Find the next 3 numbers in the pattern. _____ _____ _____

Power Practice

What do these two patterns have in common?

Name _____

In and Out

A function machine uses a rule to change numbers. Look for a pattern between the IN and OUT numbers in each table. Fill in the missing numbers. Write the rule.

1.

IN	3	9	11	6	8
OUT	6		22		16

Rule: _____

2.

IN	4	7	19	44	18
OUT		15	27	52	

Rule: _____

3.

IN	55	38	72	61	80
OUT	26		43		51

Rule: _____

4.

IN	108	27	63	126	18
OUT	12		7		2

Rule: _____

Power Practice

Describe the method you used to find the rules.

Payment Plan

Your parent proposed a deal. You will wash the dishes every day for the next 5 years on the following terms.

You will get one cent the first day.
The amount you will be paid will be doubled every day.
After one month (assume a 31-day period), you will be paid nothing for the rest of the five years.

1. Does this sound like a good deal to you? Why?

2. Does this sound like a good deal for your parent? Why?

Estimate how much you will get on each day.

3. 7th day _____   **4.** 14th day _____   **5.** 31st day _____

6. If you manage your money correctly, can you make this amount of money last for 5 years?

On a separate sheet of paper, figure out the exact amounts you will get. Organize your findings so that others can understand them.

7. How good were your estimates?

8. Now, do you think this is a good deal for you?

A Sweet Treat

Equations are often used to help solve problems. A **variable** is a letter that represents the amount you are trying to find. Follow the steps to help solve this word problem.

Tranice brought a bag full of candy to her class party. The bag held 250 miniature candy bars. When Tranice got home, there were 75 candy bars left in the bag. How many candy bars did the class eat?

1. Use B as the variable in this problem. What should B represent?

B = _____

2. Use words to write an equation describing the relationship between the known and unknown values in the problem.

3. Replace the words in the sentence above with numbers and variables to make a mathematical equation.

4. Find the value of B that makes this equation true. Show how you found your answer.

5. In word problems, you should always write your answer in a complete sentence that relates back to the original problem. Complete the following sentence.

The class ate _____ candy bars.

Name _____

Alphabet Soup

In each problem, different letters stand for different numbers. Find the numbers that will make both equations true.

1. $W + Y = 8$

$3 \times Y = 18$

$W =$ _____ $Y =$ _____

2. $80 \div B = C$

$6 + C = 10$

$B =$ _____ $C =$ _____

3. $7 + K = 12$

$2 \times K = L$

$K =$ _____ $L =$ _____

4. $M - N = 22$

$M + 12 = 52$

$M =$ _____ $N =$ _____

5. $D + F = 25$

$F \div 3 = 6$

$D =$ _____ $F =$ _____

6. $5 \times P = Q$

$P + Q = 24$

$P =$ _____ $Q =$ _____

7. $48 \div T = 16$

$T \times V = 15$

$T =$ _____ $V =$ _____

8. $H + 14 = 30$

$J - H = 9$

$J =$ _____ $H =$ _____

Coordinate Graphing

The students in Room 14 are going on a scavenger hunt at Willow Lake. Each team needs to find the objects below. Give the coordinates where each object can be found.

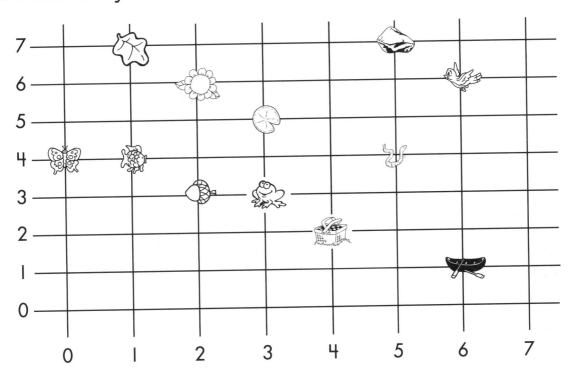

1. _____ acorn
2. _____ frog
3. _____ worm
4. _____ lily pad
5. _____ boat
6. _____ picnic basket

7. _____ rock
8. _____ butterfly
9. _____ flower
10. _____ leaf
11. _____ fish
12. _____ bird

After the scavenger hunt, the students will have a picnic. Help them get ready for the picnic by drawing the given shapes at each coordinate.

apple (5, 2)

sandwich (3, 1)

juice box (4, 3)

carrot (4, 1)

Name _____

Picture Plots

Follow the instructions below. Answer question 4.

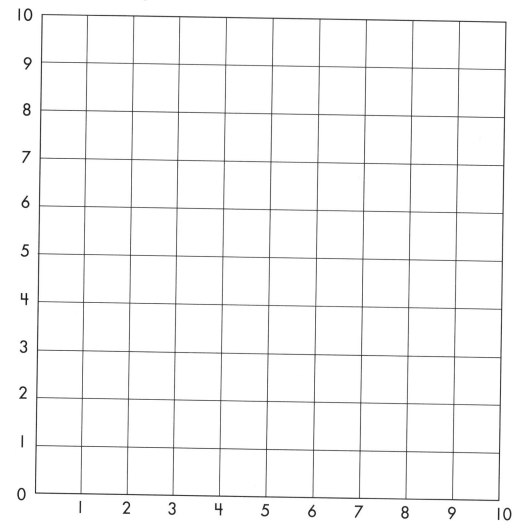

1. Plot the ordered pairs:

(2, 1)

(8, 1)

(8, 5)

(2, 5)

Connect the points in the order that you plotted them. Connect (2, 5) to (2, 1).

2. Plot the ordered pair (5, 8), and draw a line segment from (5, 8) to (2, 5). Draw another line segment from (5, 8) to (8, 5).

3. Plot the ordered pairs (6, 7), (6, 9), (7, 9), (7, 6), and connect the points in order.

4. Look at your entire drawing. What did you make?_____

Name _____

Making Money

Kanisha's dad has his own business. Over summer vacation, Kanisha is earning money by working for her dad. She helps by doing odd jobs around the office, such as filing papers and answering the phone. Her dad is paying her $5.00 an hour.

1. How much will Kanisha make in a week if she works 2 hours? _____

   How much will she earn in 3 hours? _____

2. Fill in the table to show how much money Kanisha will make in a week if she works the given number of hours.

# of hours	0	1	2	3	4	5	6
amt. earned							

3. Make a coordinate graph to show the relationship between the number of hours Kanisha works and how much money she earns.

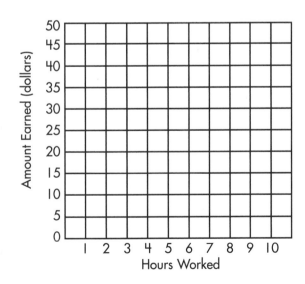

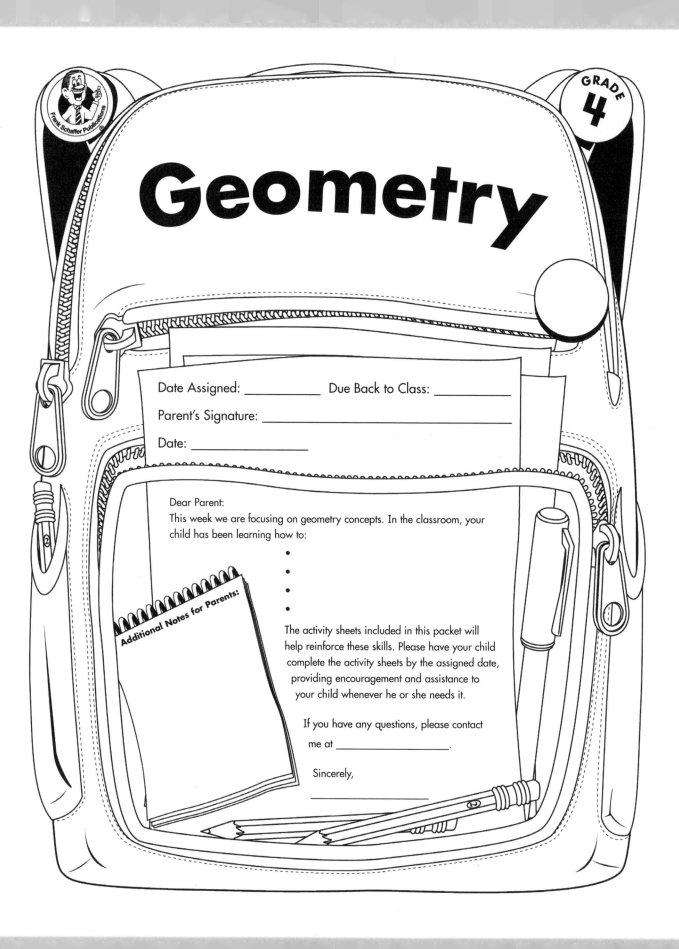

Geometry

GRADE 4

Date Assigned: _____ Due Back to Class: _____

Parent's Signature: _____

Date: _____

Dear Parent:

This week we are focusing on geometry concepts. In the classroom, your child has been learning how to:

- •
- •
- •
- •

The activity sheets included in this packet will help reinforce these skills. Please have your child complete the activity sheets by the assigned date, providing encouragement and assistance to your child whenever he or she needs it.

If you have any questions, please contact me at _____.

Sincerely,

_____

Additional Notes for Parents:

Name _____

Lines, Line Segments, and Rays

Letters are used in geometry to identify a particular figure.

A **line** goes on forever in both directions. It is drawn with an arrow on either end.	A **line segment** is a specific portion of a line. It has two endpoints.	A **ray** goes on forever in one direction from a fixed point. It is drawn with one endpoint and one arrow.
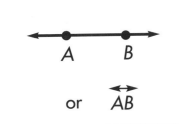 or $\overleftrightarrow{AB}$	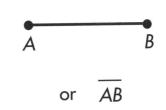 or $\overline{AB}$	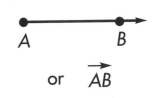 or $\overrightarrow{AB}$

Match the names to the correct drawing.

1. $\overline{AB}$ and $\overrightarrow{BD}$

a.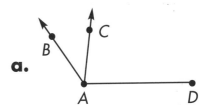

2. $\overleftrightarrow{DE}$ and $\overline{CB}$

b.

3. $\overleftrightarrow{CD}$ and $\overline{BD}$

c.

4. $\overrightarrow{AC}$ and $\overline{AD}$

d.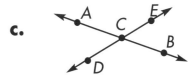

5. $\overleftrightarrow{EF}$ and $\overrightarrow{EG}$

e.

Name _____

A Class by Itself

Classifying Triangles by Side Lengths	**Classifying Triangles by Angle Measurements**
An **equilateral** triangle has three equal sides. An **isosceles** triangle has two equal sides. A **scalene** triangle has no equal sides.	A **right** triangle has one 90° angle. All the angles of an **acute** triangle are less than 90°. An **obtuse** triangle has one angle measure greater than 90°.

1. Measure the sides of each triangle. Write *equilateral, isosceles,* or *scalene* on the first line. Measure the angles of each triangle. Write *acute, obtuse,* or *right* on the second line.

a.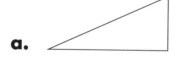

_____

_____

b.

_____

_____

c.

_____

_____

d.

_____

_____

e.

_____

_____

f.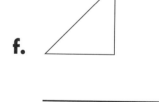

_____

_____

g.

_____

_____

h.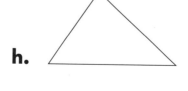

_____

_____

i.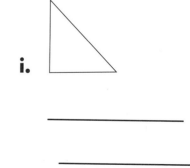

_____

_____

Describing Quadrilaterals

Complete each description of the figure drawn using the following terms.
Terms can be used more than once.

right	acute	obtuse
parallel	perpendicular	
equal	unequal	

1. A quadrilateral with 3 _____ angles

and _____ sides.

2. A quadrilateral with _____ angles and 2 pairs

of sides that are _____ .

3. A quadrilateral with 2 _____ angles and

2 _____ angles.

4. A quadrilateral with _____ sides that

form _____ angles.

5. A quadrilateral with one pair of _____ sides.

Power Practice

Write a description that uses the term *perpendicular* for the quadrilateral in
question 2.

Pyramids and Prisms

Pyramids are three-dimensional shapes with the following characteristics:
- one base shaped like a polygon
- triangular faces
- a point on one end

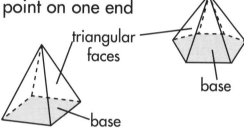

triangular faces

base

Prisms are three-dimensional shapes with the following characteristics:
- two identical bases shaped like polygons
- rectangular faces

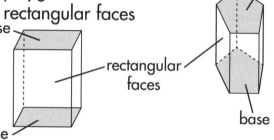

base

rectangular faces

base

base

base

Next to each shape below, write *prism*, *pyramid*, or *neither* to show what type of three-dimensional object it is. Be prepared to explain your choices.

1.

_____

2.

_____

3.

_____

4.

_____

5.

_____

6.

_____

7.

_____

8.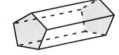

_____

9.

_____

Classifying Prisms

Prisms can be divided into several different categories. Look at each group of prisms. Circle the prism that is different from the others in its group.

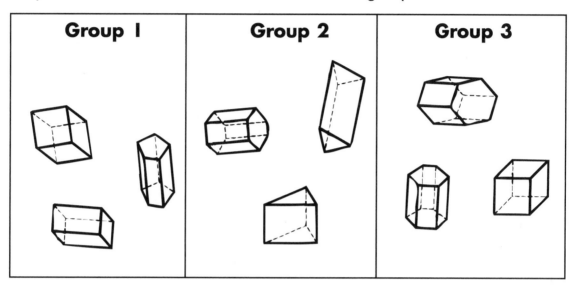

1. For each group above, write a sentence describing how the circled shape is different from the others.

   Group 1:_____

   Group 2:_____

   Group 3:_____

2. What characteristic is the same for each prism in the group, but different from the prisms in other groups?
   Hint: Compare bases of the prisms.

   Group 1:_____

   Group 2:_____

   Group 3:_____

Faces and Edges

A **face** is the flat surface of a solid figure.
The place where two faces of a solid figure meet is an **edge**.

edge → face

Complete the table.

Solid Figure	Number of Faces	Number of Edges	Number of Vertices	Shape(s) of Faces
1. cube				
2. rectangular prism				
3. triangular prism				
4. triangular pyramid				
5. square pyramid				

Congruency and Symmetry

Look at the two shapes in the box. Are the two triangles congruent?

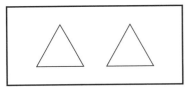

Two shapes are **congruent** if they are the same size and same shape.

Now, look at the heart in the box.

Is the heart symmetrical? Does the heart have a line of symmetry? A figure is **symmetrical** if both of its halves are congruent. A line of symmetry is the fold line that shows where the shape should be folded for the halves to be congruent. *Congruency* and *symmetry* are both words used to describe shapes.

1. What does the word *congruent* mean?

_____

_____

2. What does the word *symmetry* mean?

_____

_____

3. Are the shapes in the box congruent? _____

4. Draw an outdoor object that has a line of symmetry.

5. Draw two congruent shapes.

Name _____

Create Congruent Figures

Create three congruent figures for each figure shown using a slide, flip, and turn.

Slide	**Flip**	**Turn**

1.   _____ _____ _____

2.   _____ _____ _____

3. 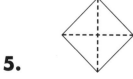 _____ _____ _____

4. 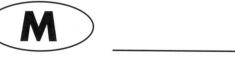 _____ _____ _____

5. _____ _____ _____

Lines of Symmetry

Draw all lines of symmetry for each figure. Tell how many lines of symmetry you drew.

1.

2.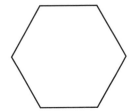

3.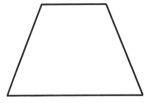

_____   _____   _____

4.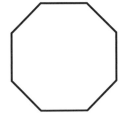

5.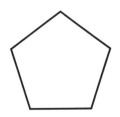

6.

_____   _____   _____

Point Symmetry

A figure that is turned about a point and looks exactly like itself before one complete rotation (360 degrees) has **point symmetry**.

Point symmetry is also called *rotational symmetry*.

Decide if each figure has point symmetry. Write *yes* or *no*.

1.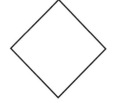

_____

2.

_____

3.

_____

4.

_____

5.

_____

6.

_____

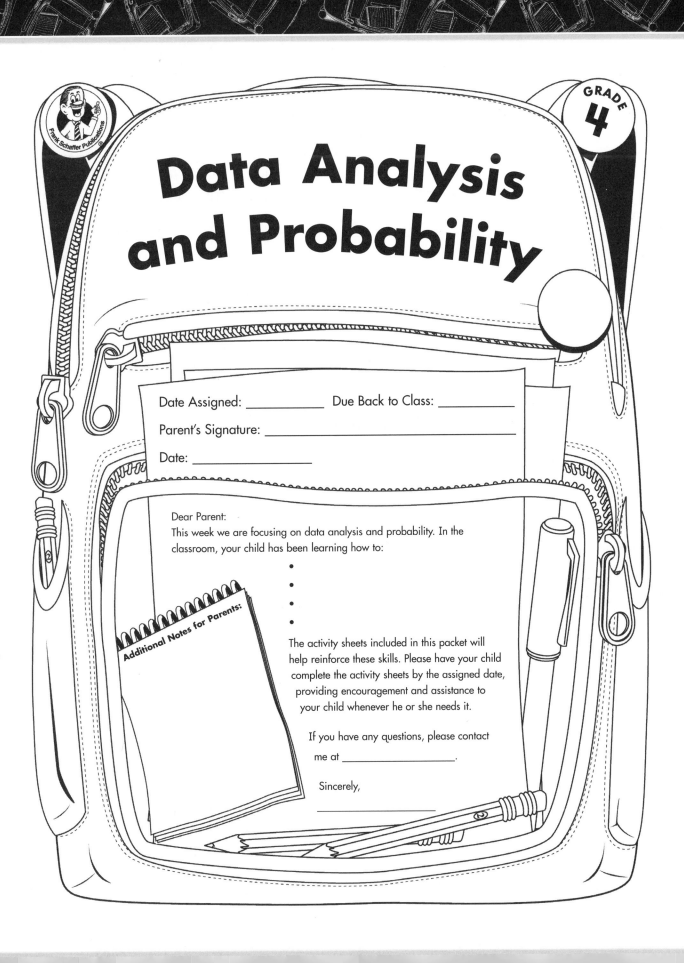

Data Analysis and Probability

GRADE 4

Date Assigned: _____ Due Back to Class: _____

Parent's Signature: _____

Date: _____

Additional Notes for Parents:

Dear Parent:

This week we are focusing on data analysis and probability. In the classroom, your child has been learning how to:

- •
- •
- •
- •

The activity sheets included in this packet will help reinforce these skills. Please have your child complete the activity sheets by the assigned date, providing encouragement and assistance to your child whenever he or she needs it.

If you have any questions, please contact me at _____.

Sincerely,

_____

Pictograph

A **pictograph** uses a symbol or picture to represent numbers on a graph. The key will tell you the number that each picture represents. Use the pictograph below to answer the questions.

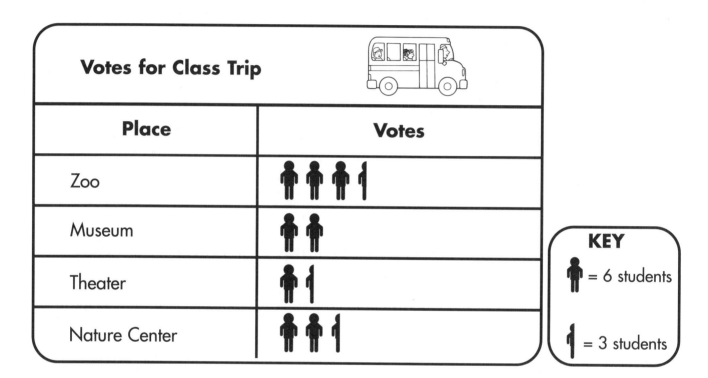

Use the pictograph to answer the questions below.

1. What is the total number of students who voted? _____

2. Which place received the least votes? _____

3. How many more students voted for the zoo than the theater? _____

4. Twelve students were absent the day of the vote. If 6 of them vote for the museum, and 6 of them vote for the theater, will that change the winning vote for the class trip? _____

5. Which place received the most votes? _____

Line Plot

A **line plot** displays data along a number line.

Each student in Mr. Himebaugh's science class worked on a science fair project. The line plot shows how many hours the students spent working on their projects. Use the line plot to answer each question.

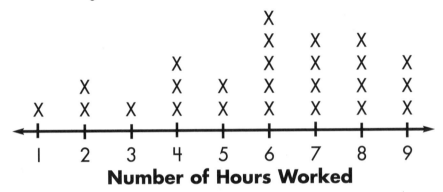

Number of Hours Worked

1. How many students are in Mr. Himebaugh's class? _____

2. How many students worked for exactly 8 hours? _____

3. How many students worked for at least 7 hours? _____

4. How many students worked no more than 4 hours? _____

Power Practice

What length of hours worked was most common in Mr. Himebaugh's class?

Make a Bar Graph

Make a bar graph using the data in the tally chart. Be sure to include a scale, the labels, and a title.

Favorite Type of Juice		
Type of Drink	**Tally**	**Number**
Apple Juice	ЖІІІ	8
Grape Juice	ЖІІ	7
Orange Juice	ЖІ	6
Cranberry Juice	ІІ	2

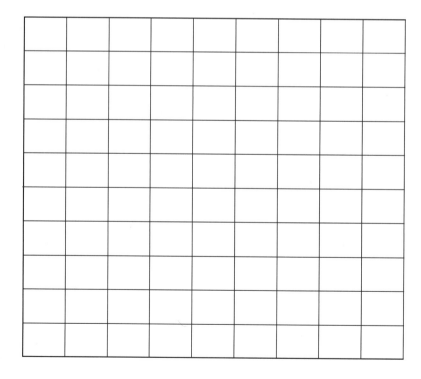

Stem and Leaf Plot

Stem and leaf plots show information. They are most often used to compare information. They are organized with a "stem," showing all the digits in a number except the "leaves," which shows the digit in the ones place. The stem and leaf plot below shows the amount of time Mary spent playing cards on her balcony during a five-day period. The blank spaces in the leaf column mean there were no numbers with the digits 6, 7, 8, 9, and 11 in the tens/hundreds place.

Amount of Time Mary Spent Playing Cards

Stem	Leaf
2	9
3	4
4	7
5	1
6	
7	
8	
9	
10	0
11	

1. What is shown as the "stem"?

_____

2. What was the average amount of time Mary spent playing cards on her balcony?

_____

3. What was the least amount of time that Mary spent playing cards on her balcony?

_____

4. What was the most time that Mary spent playing cards on her balcony?

_____

Median, Mode, and Range

The **median** is the number in the middle when a group of numbers is arranged in order from least to greatest.

The **mode** is the number that occurs most often.

Example:
20 25 26 26 26 26 **32** 33 34 34 35 37 39

The median is **32**.
The mode is **26**.
The range is **19**.

To find the **range**, subtract the least number from the greatest.

For each of the following number groups, list the median, mode, and range. For some problems, you will need to rearrange the numbers in numerical order first.

1. 13 14 14 14 15 17 17 19 21

median _____

mode _____

range _____

2. 50 52 52 52 53 56 58 58 60

median _____

mode _____

range _____

3. 6 9 10 12 14 14 15

median _____

mode _____

range _____

4. 82 86 91 80 82 82 89

median _____

mode _____

range _____

5. 71 73 73 73 74 76 79

median _____

mode _____

range _____

6. 5 4 4 8 3 2 1

median _____

mode _____

range _____

7. 31 32 33 34 35 36 36

median _____

mode _____

range _____

8. 10 32 27 25 37 16 25

median _____

mode _____

range _____

Means in the World

Find the mean of each data set.

1.

Fast Animals	
Animal	**Speed**
cheetah	70 mph
lion	50 mph
zebra	40 mph
rabbit	35 mph

_____

2.

Tallest Buildings	
Building	**Height**
Petronas Towers	1,483 feet
Sears Tower	1,450 feet
Jin Mao Building	1,381 feet

_____

3.

High Rollercoasters	
Rollercoaster	**Height**
Millennium Force	310 feet
Fujiyama	259 feet
Goliath	255 feet
Son of Beast	218 feet
Pepsi Max Big One	214 feet

_____

4.

Diameter of Planets	
Planet	**Diameter**
Mercury	3,032 miles
Venus	7,521 miles
Earth	7,926 miles
Mars	4,213 miles

_____

Way Out There

Sometimes, a set of data contains a value that is not typical of the other values in the set.

This type of data point is an **outlier**.

Identify the outlier in each set of data.

1.

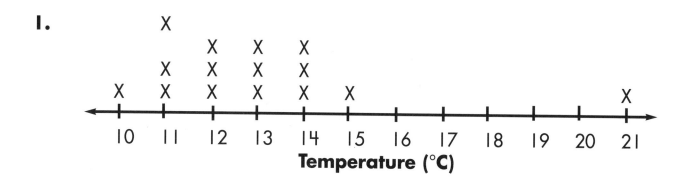

Temperature (°C)

_____

2.

Age (years)								
22	41	21	56	33	41	63	38	36
35	50	49	27	44	5	38	45	28

_____

Power Practice

Do you think a data set can have more than one outlier? Explain.

Probability

The **probability** of an event is the chance that it will occur. Probabilities are often expressed as fractions. The probability of an event ranges from 0 (impossible) to 1 (certain).

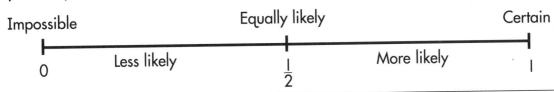

Impossible   Equally likely   Certain

Less likely   More likely

0          $\frac{1}{2}$ 1

Answer each question.

1. Suppose the probability of pulling a blue chip from a bag is $\frac{1}{4}$, and the probability of pulling a red chip is $\frac{1}{2}$. Which event is more likely? Explain.

   _____

2. Kendra rolls two number cubes while playing a board game. The probability that both number cubes show an odd number is $\frac{1}{4}$. The probability that both cubes show the same number is $\frac{1}{6}$. Which event is more likely? Explain.

   _____

3. A cookie jar contains 6 sugar cookies, 4 chocolate chip cookies, and 8 peanut butter cookies. Which type of cookie has the greatest probability of being selected? Explain.

   _____

Power Practice

Probability is usually expressed as a fraction, but it can be written in different ways. Name two other ways that probability can be expressed.

Spinner Fun

Probability = $\dfrac{\text{\# items in that category}}{\text{total items}}$

Look at the spinner. Write the color that matches each probability below.

1. $\dfrac{3}{8}$ _____

2. $\dfrac{1}{4}$ _____

3. $\dfrac{1}{8}$ _____

_____

_____

4. 0 _____

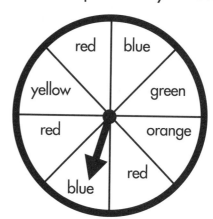

5. Explain how you found the answers for problems 1–4.

Look at the spinner. What is the probability that the arrow will land on—

6. a shape? _____

7. a number? _____

8. a number or a shape? _____

9. a hexagon? _____

10. a triangle? _____

11. an even number? _____

12. an odd number? _____

Name _____

Pick a Card

Nancy has 7 letter cards face down on her desk. She picks 1 card at random. Find the probability of each event.

1. picking a card with a T

_____

2. picking a card with an M or an O

_____

3. picking a card with a vowel

_____

4. picking a card with a consonant

_____

5. picking a card that has a letter made only with curves

_____

6. picking a card that has a letter from her name

_____

Power Practice

What letter could you add to the end of the word OUTCOME (and still have a word) so that picking a vowel would have the same probability as picking a consonant?

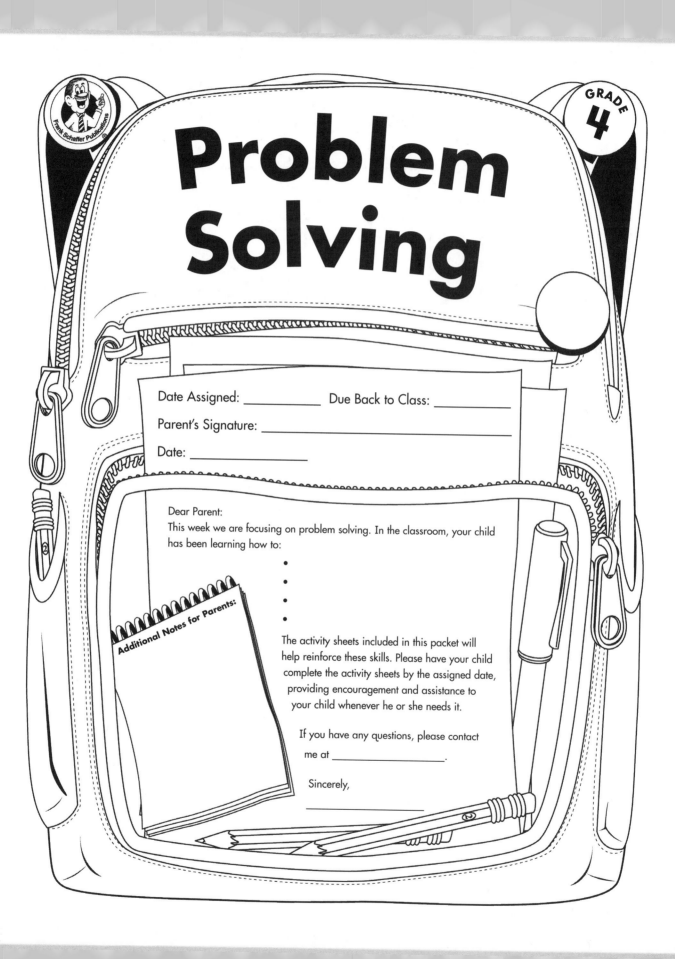

Problem Solving

GRADE 4

Date Assigned: _____ Due Back to Class: _____

Parent's Signature: _____

Date: _____

Additional Notes for Parents:

Dear Parent:

This week we are focusing on problem solving. In the classroom, your child has been learning how to:

- •
- •
- •
- •

The activity sheets included in this packet will help reinforce these skills. Please have your child complete the activity sheets by the assigned date, providing encouragement and assistance to your child whenever he or she needs it.

If you have any questions, please contact me at _____.

Sincerely,

_____

Find the Number

Read each riddle and identify the number. Write the standard and expanded forms on the line.

1. I am a 6-digit odd number between 125,939 and 125,970. My digits have a sum of 28. No digit is repeated. What number am I?

   standard form: _____

   expanded form: _____

2. I have 5 odd digits. The ones, hundreds, and ten thousands digits are the same. The tens digit is the sum of the 3 identical digits. The total sum of the 5 digits is 23. What number am I?

   standard form: _____

   expanded form: _____

3. I am a 6-digit odd number. My digits add to 33. Each digit is 1 less than the previous digit. What number am I?

   standard form: _____

   expanded form: _____

4. I am a 6-digit even number between 350,000 and 750,000. The sum of my digits is 27. The digits in the ones period are the same. The digits in the thousands period are the same. What number am I?

   standard form: _____

   expanded form: _____

5. I am a 5-digit number with each digit 2 less than the previous digit. My digits add to 25. What number am I?

   standard form: _____

   expanded form: _____

6. I have 6 digits. The digits in the thousands period are 1 less than the previous digit. The ones digit is 1 more than the hundred thousands digit. The tens digit is double the ten thousands digit. The hundreds digit, which is 9, is 3 times the one thousands digit. What number am I?

   standard form: _____

   expanded form: _____

Name _____

Choose Your Operation

Read each problem. Circle the function you would use to solve it. Explain to a friend how you decided which operation to choose. You do not have to solve the problem.

+ − x ÷   **1.**   The red bike costs $154.78. The blue bike costs $132.50. How much more does the red bike cost?

+ − x ÷   **2.**   The administration wants to assign 2,082 students to 6 schools. How many students in each school?

+ − x ÷   **3.**   15,860 beads were put into 65 bags. How many beads are in each bag?

+ − x ÷   **4.**   Mike bought 4 new shirts. Each shirt cost $15.88. How much were the shirts before tax?

+ − x ÷   **5.**   There are 345 students at Valley Elementary and 409 students at Hilltop Elementary. How many students at both schools?

+ − x ÷   **6.**   Jackie made a 74-minute long distance telephone call. Her mother charged her the 6¢ a minute from the phone bill. How much did Jackie owe her mother?

+ − x ÷   **7.**   Tara reads 13 pages each night. How long does it take her to finish her 195-page book?

+ − x ÷   **8.**   The container holds enough mix to make 18 servings of mashed potatoes. If each serving needs 3 scoops of mix, how many scoops of mix are in the container?

+ − x ÷   **9.**   Matthew is required to practice his horn for 180 minutes a week. He has already practiced for 124 minutes. How many minutes does he still need to practice?

+ − x ÷ **10.**   Jamal's family collects state quarters. They have 127 quarters in one container and 235 quarters in another container. How many quarters do they have?

Power Practice

Solve the problems on this page.

Use Your Head

Estimate and solve the problem in your head. Write your answer. Then, solve using paper and pencil. You may use any strategies you are comfortable using.

1. Danielle has 3 quarters in her pocket. She has 5 dimes in her backpack. She wants to buy a bag of chips and a pop for $1.09. Does she have enough money? _____

2. Emily bought a package of 72 pencils with holiday toppers. She wants to give one to each person in her classroom, her brother's classroom, and her sister's classroom. She has 26 students in her class, her brother has 24 students in his class, and her sister has 25 students in her class. Does she have enough pencils for every person? _____

3. Miguel wants to purchase a binder for $3.52, a pack of pencils for 84¢, and 6 folders for 24¢ each. He has $5.00. Does he have enough money? _____

4. Ramiro is collecting food package points. If he collects 475 points, he will have enough to order a computer game. He collected 57 in June, 107 in July, 230 in August, and 61 in September. Does he have enough to place his order?

   _____

5. Maria needs enough donuts for two classrooms of 26. Donuts come in packages of 12. If she buys 4 packages, does she have enough or does she need to buy one more? _____

6. Brent needs 2,647 toothpicks to complete a sculpture. He has an open box with 847 toothpicks in it. He found a box at the store with 500 toothpicks in it. What is the smallest number of boxes he needs to complete his project? _____

Addition Problem Solving

Macy's mom works at a music store. Macy helped her mom keep track of CDs at the store. Write the answer to each problem on the line.

1. There are 762 CD titles listed in the computer. Macy enters 292 new titles into the computer. What is the total number of CD titles listed now?_____

2. One day, 278 CDs were sold. The next day, 183 CDs were sold. What is the total number of CDs sold in those two days?_____

3. The music store had 757 customers last month and 662 customers this month. How many customers did the store have all together in those two months?_____

Todd's mom has a special plan for his birthday. Write the answer to each problem on the line.

4. Todd's mom took him and a friend to a water park for his birthday. His friend, Steve, walked 3 blocks to get to Todd's house. Then, Todd, his mom, and Steve walked 6 more blocks to the water park. How many blocks did Steve walk by the time he got back home later that night? _____

5. Mom, Todd, and Steve were standing in line at the ticket counter. There were 8 people standing in front of them and 4 people standing behind them. How many people were standing in line?_____

6. An adult ticket costs $12.00. A child's ticket costs half that much. Todd and Steve are charged the child's ticket price. How much did Mom pay for the tickets to the water park? Write how you would find the answer to this problem.

_____

_____

Subtraction Problem Solving

Ms. Ramon's gym class is practicing for the Fitness Challenge. There are two teams with four students on each team. To complete the challenge, each team must complete the following exercises:

100	sit-ups
100	push-ups
120	jumping jacks
2,000	meters of running

Fill in the totals for the tables below. Then, answer the questions.

Team 1

Student	Sit-Ups	Push-Ups	Jumping Jacks	Meters Run
Mariana	24	21	23	300
Jacob	17	18	25	500
Carlos	25	23	18	250
Emily	25	20	17	450
Team Total				

Team 2

Student	Sit-Ups	Push-Ups	Jumping Jacks	Meters Run
Samuel	25	24	17	300
Natalie	18	19	25	500
Jonah	21	16	25	450
Kanesha	18	25	21	500
Team Total				

1. How many push-ups does team one have to do to finish the contest? _____

2. What is the total number of jumping jacks remaining for team two? _____

3. Which team has the most sit-ups left to do? _____

4. Which team has the least number of meters left to run? _____

Multiplication Problem Solving

The students at P.S. 134 are having a book sale. They are arranging the books into categories and stacking them on tables. Read the following problems and write your answers on the lines. Use what you know about multiplication to solve the problems.

1. Josh sorted books about sports. When he was finished, he had 8 stacks of 6 books each. How many sports books in all were at the sale?

_____

2. The largest category of books was fiction. Rebecca had 12 stacks with 10 books in each stack. How many fiction books were at the sale?

_____

3. The book sale was in the gym. The students set up tables into 9 rows with 4 tables in each row. What was the total number of tables in the gym?

_____

4. The customers were excited by the sale. They lined up to pay for their books. There were 5 lines with 17 customers in each line. How many customers were waiting to pay?

_____

5. The table with picture books for children was a mess. Hee-Jung sorted them into stacks. When she was finished, she had 12 stacks with 5 books in each stack. How many picture books were there at the sale?

_____

6. When the sale was over, the students counted the money. Bruno counted the five-dollar bills. He had 14 five-dollar bills. How much money did Bruno have?

_____

Multiple–Step Problems

1. There are 26 scouts in Derek's troop. Two of the scouts are 8 years old. There are twice as many 10-year-old scouts as there are 9-year-old scouts. How many 9-year-old scouts are there? Show your work.

2. Antwan's mother brought strawberries to his scout meeting. There were 24 boys and 3 group leaders. She brought 185 strawberries, and there were 20 left over. If the leaders ate 7 strawberries each, and each scout ate the same number of strawberries, how many did each scout eat? Show your work.

3. At the scouting awards, 58 achievement arrows were awarded. If Yoshi got 3 arrows and the other 25 scouts got at least 2, what is the largest number of scouts besides Yoshi who could have gotten more than 2? Show your work.

4. At scout camp, there were 11 scouts in each cabin. There are 8 cabins. Half the scouts will be going canoeing. Each canoe holds 2 people. How many canoes will be needed? Show your work.

Name _____

Smart Shopper

1. Theo goes shopping for cereal. The same cereal is available in 2 different sizes. A 16 oz. box costs $4.37. A 20 oz. box costs $5.22. Which would be the best buy?

   a. If 16 oz. cost $4.37, 1 oz. would cost $4.37 ÷ 16 = _____.

   b. If 20 oz. cost $5.22, 1 oz. would cost _____ = _____.

   c. The _____ oz. box would be the better buy.

2. Kiwadin could buy a 3 lb. bag of oranges for $1.69. There are a dozen oranges in the bag. He could buy oranges separately for $0.20 each. Should he buy the oranges separately or in a bag? Explain.

3. Charles bought a box of 50 baseball cards for $25.00. His friend Deshawn likes to buy cards in packs of 10 for $4.00 each. Which boy got the better buy? Explain.

Power Practice

How do you find the price per ounce if you know the price for 12 ounces?

Riddles

Read the riddles to determine the coins (combinations of fifty-cent pieces, quarters, dimes, nickels, or pennies). Use real coins or sketches to assist you.

1. I have 12 coins worth $1.05. The coins include 3 different kinds. What are the coins?

2. I have 6 silver coins. Their value is $1.90. What are the coins?

3. My 3 types of coins total 37¢. I have fewer than 4, but more than 1, of each coin. What are the coins?

4. My 14 coins total $2.00. I have at least 1 of each of the 5 coins. What are the coins?

5. My 9 coins are worth 60¢. Not one is a nickel. What are the coins?

6. I have the same number of each coin in my pocket. Their total value is $1.30. What are the coins?

7. One coin type is in my pocket. I have between 9 and 30 coins. Their total value is $2.00. What are the coins?

8. Choose an amount between $1.00 and $2.00. Show 2 ways to make the amount. Choose one and write a riddle for it.

_____

_____

_____

Name _____

Money

Read the directions. Give the total amount of spending money.

1. Melissa has 6 coins. One-half $\left(\frac{1}{2}\right)$ are dimes, two-sixths $\left(\frac{2}{6}\right)$ are pennies, and the rest are nickels. How much does Melissa have?

_____

2. Jamal has 9 coins. One-third $\left(\frac{1}{3}\right)$ are half-dollars, four-ninths $\left(\frac{4}{9}\right)$ are nickels, and the rest are dimes. How much does Jamal have?

_____

3. Samantha has 4 coins. One-fourth $\left(\frac{1}{4}\right)$ are quarters, one-half $\left(\frac{1}{2}\right)$ are pennies, and the rest are dimes. How much does Samantha have? _____

4. Mariana has 8 coins. One-half $\left(\frac{1}{2}\right)$ are pennies, one-fourth $\left(\frac{1}{4}\right)$ are nickels, and the rest are half-dollars. How much does Mariana have? _____

5. Brian has 12 coins. One-half $\left(\frac{1}{2}\right)$ are quarters, one-third $\left(\frac{1}{3}\right)$ are dimes, and the rest are pennies. How much does Brian have? _____

6. Michael has 10 coins. Three-tenths $\left(\frac{3}{10}\right)$ are dimes, one-fifth $\left(\frac{1}{5}\right)$ are quarters, and the rest are half-dollars. How much does Michael have? _____

Answer Key

Place Value 10
1. 54,671—seven tens
2. 354,942—nine hundreds
3. 203,203—two hundred thousands
4. 67,881—seven thousands
5. 495,463—six tens
6. 485,751—eight ten thousands
7. 763,389—three hundreds
8. 892,855—five ones
9. 103,254—one hundred thousand

Pull It Apart 11
1. 3,000,000 + 200,000 + 70,000 + 1,000 + 300 + 80 + 9
2. 5,000,000 + 500,000 + 4,000 + 900 + 20 + 8
3. 600,000 + 4,000 + 500 + 40 + 5
4. 200 + 40 + 1
5. 400,000 + 80,000 + 7,000 + 600 + 80 + 9
6. 30,000 + 4,000 + 900
7. 1,000 + 100 + 60 + 2
8. 900,000 + 40,000 + 700 + 60 + 1
9. 8,000,000 + 900,000 + 20,000 + 1,000 + 200 + 60
10. 700 + 50 + 3

Power Practice:
1. three million, two hundred and seventy-one thousand, three hundred eighty-nine
2. five million, five hundred and four thousand, nine hundred twenty-eight
3. six hundred and four thousand, five hundred forty-five
4. two hundred forty-one
5. four hundred and eighty-seven thousand, six hundred eighty-nine
6. thirty-four thousand, nine hundred
7. one thousand, one hundred sixty-two
8. nine hundred and forty thousand, seven hundred sixty-one
9. eight million, nine hundred and twenty-one thousand, two hundred sixty
10. seven hundred fifty-three

Missing Information 12
1. standard form: 5,413

expanded form: 5,000 + 400 + 10 + 3
circle: odd
2. word form: two thousand, five hundred sixty-eight
expanded form: 2,000 + 500 + 60 + 8
circle: even
3. word form: seven thousand, five hundred two
standard form: 7,502
circle: even
4. standard form: 3,281
expanded form: 3,000 + 200 + 80 + 1
circle: odd
5. word form: two thousand, eighty-five
expanded form: 2,000 + 80 + 5
circle: odd

Comparisons 13
1. <   2. <   3. =   4. >   5. >
6. >   7. <   8. >   9. <   10. >
11. <   12. >   13. >   14. <   15. <
16. >   17. =   18. >   19. <   20. <

Power Practice: Students' tally charts should indicate that 9 greater than signs were used, 9 less than signs were used, and 2 equal signs were used.

The Next Number Is 14
1. 1,586, 1,696, 1,806 (+110)
2. 34,262, 34,162, 34,062 (−100)
3. 390,025, 392,525, 395,025 (+2,500)
4. 1,200,245, 1,300,245, 1,400,245 (+100,000)
5. 566,352, 565,352, 564,352 (−1,000)

Power Practice: Students' number lines and explanations will vary.

Rounding 15
1. 480   2. 120   3. 910
4. 124,500   5. 72,190   6. 4,500,000
7. 74,000   8. 4,300,000 9. 152,600
10. 5,800,000 11. 400,000   12. 2,940,000
13. 1,645,300 14. 687,000   15. 2,672,500
16. 37,000   17. 3,680,000 18. 8,032,500
19. 7,000   20. 2,100,000 21. 3,840,000
22. 249,000   23. 40,000   24. 1,000,000

Answer Key

The Right Place 16
1. 498,765,321 **2.** 412,356,789
3. 976,584,321 **4.** 123,456,789
5. 986,574,132

Finding Factors 17
1. **a.** the last digit is even
 b. the last digit is 5 or 0
 c. the last digit is 0
2. A number has a factor of 3 if the sum of its digits is a multiple of 3.
3. A number has a factor of 9 if the sum of its digits is a multiple of 9.
4. 4 is a factor of: 128; 2,464; 272; 388; 2,300; 4,512. Yes, the trick always works (if you think of any number ending in 00 as being "100," which is divisible by 4).

Multiples 18
1. 3, 6, 9, 12, 15, 18, 21, 24
 4, 8, 12, 16, 20, 24, 28, 32
 6, 12, 18, 24, 30, 36, 42, 48
2. 12 and 24   **3.** 12
4. **a.** 15   **b.** 14   **c.** 18
 d. 24   **e.** 20   **f.** 36

Positively Prime 19
1. 2 is the only even prime number. All other even numbers have a factor of 2.
2. Every prime number, except 2, is odd. But, not all odd numbers are prime. 9 is odd and has a factor of 3.
3. No. The product will automatically have 2 additional factors besides itself and 1.
4. The multiplication table shows many numbers that are not prime. If a number is found in the table (so long as it is not in the "1 x" row or column), then it is **not** prime.
5. **a–e.** no   **f.** Answers may vary.
 g. 143 ÷ 11 = 13   **h.** No.
6. 2, 3, 5, 7, 11, 13, 17, 19, 23, 29, 31, 37, 41, 43, 47, 53, 59, 61, 67, 71, 73, 79, 83, 89, and 97

To the Drawing Board 21
Diagrams will vary, but must meet criteria given.

Fractions on the Number Line 22
1–6. Each fraction is placed on the given number line near the correct place. Spaces between fractional parts should be about equal for each number line.

Greater Than, Less Than, or Equal? . . . 23
1. Sketches should match fractions.
2. Fractions should be placed on number line.
3. **a.** <   **b.** >   **c.** =
 d. >   **e.** <   **f.** <
 g. >   **h.** <   **i.** >

The Same Size Piece 24
1. 4 **2.** 3 **3.** 8 **4.** 3 **5.** 16
6. 6 **7.** 4 **8.** 12 **9.** 21

Explanations will vary.
10. No. $\frac{2}{3} = \frac{3}{6}$; $\frac{5}{6}$ is larger.
11. Yes. Both are equal to $\frac{1}{2}$.
12. No. Fiona practiced longer. $\frac{3}{4} = \frac{15}{20}$; this is less than $\frac{16}{20}$.
13. No. $\frac{3}{4} = \frac{6}{8}$; Joseph used more.
14. Yes. Both are equal to $\frac{3}{4}$.

Fractions in Lowest Terms 25
1. $\frac{1}{4}$ **2.** $\frac{2}{5}$ **3.** $\frac{1}{5}$ **4.** $\frac{3}{5}$ **5.** $\frac{1}{4}$
6. $\frac{3}{4}$ **7.** $\frac{7}{8}$ **8.** $\frac{1}{2}$ **9.** $\frac{3}{4}$ **10.** $\frac{1}{2}$
11. $\frac{3}{5}$ **12.** $\frac{2}{3}$ **13.** $\frac{1}{2}$ **14.** $\frac{1}{2}$ **15.** $\frac{1}{4}$
16. $\frac{3}{4}$ **17.** $\frac{1}{2}$ **18.** $\frac{1}{6}$

Hundredths 26
1. 0.04, $\frac{4}{100}$ **2.** 0.08, $\frac{8}{100}$ **3.** 0.06, $\frac{6}{100}$
4. 0.13, $\frac{13}{100}$ **5.** 0.19, $\frac{19}{100}$ **6.** 0.41, $\frac{41}{100}$
7. 0.89, $\frac{89}{100}$ **8.** 5.03, $5\frac{3}{100}$ **9.** 6.01, $6\frac{1}{100}$
10. 27.72, $27\frac{72}{100}$ **11.** 3,542.06; $3,542\frac{6}{100}$
12. 900.05, $900\frac{5}{100}$ **13.** 2,701.02; $2,701\frac{2}{100}$
14. 365.11, $365\frac{11}{100}$ **15.** 5 squares shaded
16. 3 squares shaded **17.** 18 squares shaded
18. 54 squares shaded **19.** 87 squares shaded
20. 29 squares shaded

Answer Key

Match Them Up 27
1. **e**, 0.4   2. **j**, 0.6   3. **g**, 4.59
4. **a**, 6,000.11 5. **i**, 5.2   6. **l**, 0.98
7. **c**, 8.04   8. **b**, 70.1   9. **h**, 901.22
10. **k**, 0.54   11. **d**, 49.3   12. **f**, 1,010.04

Decimal Rounding 28
1. 5.2   2. 18.4   3. 1.0
4. 148.2   5. 30.0   6. 5.1
7. 0.23   8. 63.48   9. 29.07
10. 0.08   11. 967.50   12. 6.38
13. 0.006   14. 0.265   15. 3.401
16. 63.043   17. 541.730   18. 700.928

Pleading the Fifth 29
1. **a.** $\frac{1}{5}$ **b.** Students should have $\frac{2}{10}$ shaded.
   c. $\frac{2}{10} = \frac{20}{100}$. **d.** 20%
2. $\frac{2}{5} = \frac{1}{5} + \frac{1}{5} = 20\% + 20\% = 40\%$
3. $\frac{3}{5} = 60\%$; $\frac{4}{5} = 80\%$
Power Practice: $\frac{2}{3} \approx 33\% + 33\% \approx 66\%$

What Part of the Whole? 30
1. **a.** $\frac{4}{10}$,   **b.** 0.4,   **c.** 40%
2. **a.** 30%,   **b.** 0.3,   **c.** $\frac{3}{10}$
3. **a.** $\frac{6}{10}$,   **b.** 60%,   **c.** 0.6
4. **a.** $\frac{45}{100}$,   **b.** 0.45,   **c.** 45%
5. **a.** $\frac{41}{100}$,   **b.** 0.41,   **c.** 41%
6. **a.** 29%, **b.** $\frac{6}{100}$, **c.** 0.47, **d.** $\frac{18}{100}$ and 0.18

Addition and Subtraction Families 32
1. 7 + 8 = 15, 8 + 7 = 15,
   15 − 7 = 8, 15 − 8 = 7
2. 321 + 246 = 567, 246 + 321 = 567,
   567 − 321 = 246, 567 − 246 = 321
3. missing: 69,
   69 + 43 = 112, 43 + 69 = 112,
   112 − 69 = 43, 112 − 43 = 69
4. missing: 877,
   764 + 113 = 877, 113 + 764 = 877,
   877 − 764 = 113, 877 − 113 = 764

Adjust the Space 33
1. + 4, 55 − 30 = 25   2. +1, 74 − 50 = 24
3. +2, 94 − 50 = 44   4. + 3, 68 − 20 = 48
5. + 4, 88 − 60 = 28   6. +6, 96 − 30 = 66
7. + 3, 46 − 40 = 6
8. +2, 464 − 430 = 34
9. + 3, 356 − 330 = 26
10. +20, 470 − 300 = 170

Rebuilding the Pyramid 34

1.
123			
61	62		
28	33	29	
11	17	16	13
3	8	9	7	6

2.
248			
132	116		
71	61	55	
37	34	27	28
17	20	14	13	15

3.
430		
215	215	
124	91	124
86	38	53	71
70	16	22	31	40

4.
1,223			
622	601		
328	294	307	
179	149	145	162
99	80	69	76	86
62	37	43	26	50	36

5.
3882					
2,002	1,880				
974	1,028	852			
444	530	498	354		
192	252	278	220	134	
84	108	144	134	86	48
42	42	66	78	56	30	18
25	17	25	41	37	19	11	7
16	9	8	17	24	13	6	5	2

Check With the Opposite 35
1. 5,850; 5,850 + 3,364 = 9,214
2. 3,770; 3,770 + 1,559 = 5,329
3. 6,241; 6,241 − 3,458 = 2,783
4. 8,476; 8,476 − 3,649 = 4,827
5. 506; 506 + 896 = 1,402
6. 345 + 648 = 993 trading cards
   993 − 648 = 345
7. 4,071 − 1,257 = 2,814 more home team
   spectators 2,814 + 1,257 = 4,071
8. $102.34 − $45.78 = $56.56
   $56.56 + $45.78 = $102.34

Answer Key

Using Estimation **36**
1. 1,281, 500 + 800 = 1,300
2. 1,349, 600 + 800 = 1,400
3. 377, 900 – 500 = 400
4. 347, 900 – 600 = 300
5. 930, 700 + 300 = 1000
6. 357, 500 – 200 = 300
7. 10,175, 7,000 + 3,000 = 10,000
8. 6,816, 9,000 – 2,000 = 7,000
9. 3,347, 8,000 – 4,000 = 4,000
10. 8,241, 6,000 + 3,000 = 9,000
11. 879, 6,000 – 5,000 = 1,000
12. 3,708, 7,000 – 4,000 = 3,000

Power Practice: Students' explanations will vary.

Paying the Bills **37**
1. $168.49 2. $32.65
3. $32.95 4. $24.75

Decimals **38**
1. 9.4 2. 7.8 3. 10.9 4. 7.9
5. 6.9 6. 2.7 7. 1.1 8. 5.3
9. 2.5 10. 2.4 11. .48 12. .59
13. .68 14. .79 15. .99

Here Come Decimals **39**
1. 181.47 2. 47.643 3. 401.65
4. 55.17 5. 399.29 6. 21.53
7. 666.88 8. 51.158 9. 14.113
10. 37.189 11. 5.675 12. 98.228
13. shade: 401.65, 51.158, 5.675, 181.47
14. a. $\frac{4}{100}$ b. 0.4 c. 40% d. four tenths

All Together Now **40**
1. $\frac{5}{6}$ 2. $\frac{2}{4}$ 3. $\frac{7}{10}$ 4. $\frac{5}{7}$ 5. $\frac{3}{9}$
6. $\frac{4}{5}$ 7. $\frac{6}{8}$ 8. $\frac{3}{3}$ 9. $\frac{3}{4}$ 10. $\frac{7}{9}$
11. $\frac{10}{12}$ 12. $\frac{4}{6}$ 13. $\frac{2}{8}$ 14. $\frac{9}{11}$

Tossing Some Out **41**
1. $\frac{1}{3}$ 2. $\frac{3}{8}$ 3. $\frac{2}{5}$
4. $\frac{4}{10}$ or $\frac{2}{5}$ 5. $\frac{3}{6}$ or $\frac{1}{2}$ 6. $\frac{3}{4}$
7. $\frac{4}{12}$ or $\frac{1}{3}$ 8. $\frac{4}{7}$ 9. $\frac{4}{8}$ or $\frac{1}{2}$
10. $\frac{4}{9}$ 11. $\frac{5}{12}$ 12. $\frac{1}{4}$
13. $\frac{2}{10}$ or $\frac{1}{5}$ 14. $\frac{1}{2}$

Commutative and Associative Properties **43**
1. C 2. A 3. C 4. A 5. C
6. C 7. 4 x 3 = 3 x 4
8. 5 + 8 + 6 = 8 + 5 + 6 or 5 + 6 + 8
9. 7 x (4 x 3) = (7 x 4) x 3
10. 7 x (4 x 3) = (4 x 3) x 7 or 7 x (3 x 4)
11. (8 + 4) + 2 = 8 + (4 + 2)
12. 2 x (3 x 6) x 4 = (2 x 3) x 6 x 4 or
    2 x 3 x (6 x 4) or (2 x 3) x (6 x 4)

Division **44**
1. 8, Rule 1 2. 4, Rule 1
3. 0, Rule 3 4. Not possible, Rule 4
5. 1, Rule 2 6. 0, Rule 3
7. Not possible, Rule 4 8. 1, Rule 2

Distributive Property **45**
1. 2(6 + 3) = 2 x 6 + 2 x 3; 18 = 18
2. 12 + 9 = 4 x 3 + 3 x 3 = (4 + 3)3; 21 = 21
3. 4(9 – 1) = 4 x 9 – 4 x 1; 32 = 32
4. 18 – 6 = 6 x 3 – 6 x 1 = 6(3 – 1); 12 = 12
5. (15 – 3)2 = 15 x 2 – 3 x 2; 24 = 24
6. (7 + 5)8 = 7 x 8 + 5 x 8; 96 = 96
7. 25 – 15 = 5 x 5 – 3 x 5 = (5 – 3)5; 10 = 10
8. 3(5 + 6) = 3 x 5 + 3 x 6; 33 = 33
9. 8 + 12 = 4 x 2 + 4 x 3 = 4(2 + 3); 20 = 20

Multiplication and Division Families . . . **46**
1. 8 x 7 = 56, 7 x 8 = 56, 56 ÷ 7 = 8,
   56 ÷ 8 = 7
2. 8 x 24 = 192, 24 x 8 = 192, 192 ÷ 8 = 24,
   192 ÷ 24 = 8
3. missing: 73, 2 x 73 = 146, 73 x 2 = 146,
   146 ÷ 2 = 73, 146 ÷ 73 = 2
4. missing: 238, 7 x 34 = 238, 34 x 7 = 238,
   238 ÷ 7 = 34, 238 ÷ 34 = 7

Power Practice: Students' triangles and fact families will vary.

Answer Key

Groups 47

Each answer should include appropriate picture.
1. 132, 33 + 33 + 33 + 33 = 132
2. 200, 25 + 25 + 25 + 25 + 25 + 25 + 25 + 25 = 200
3. 112, 56 + 56 = 112
4. 147, 49 + 49 + 49 = 147
5. 246, 41 + 41 + 41 + 41 + 41 + 41 = 246
6. 506, 253 + 253 = 506
7. 414, 138 + 138 + 138 = 414
8. 785, 785 + 0 = 785 or 785 = 785

Multiplication 48

1. 594	**2.** 308	**3.** 1,430
4. 931	**5.** 1,176	**6.** 540
7. 1,050	**8.** 703	**9.** 1,862
10. 912	**11.** 3,416	**12.** 1,440
13. 3,108	**14.** 6,664	**15.** 2,380

More Multiplication 49

Row 1	Row 2	Row 3
32,296 (A)	64,790 (G)	22,815 (B)
5,486 (J)	35,392 (O)	41,610 (U)
55,800 (A)	35,476 (E)	67,824 (E)
37,884 (B)	57,672 (D)	24,414 (N)
19,912 (U)	39,648 (!)	45,408 (O)

Numbers in the Groups 50

Each problem also requires two different ways to fill sets.

1. 4	**2.** 6	**3.** 9	**4.** 7	**5.** 7
6. 8	**7.** 8	**8.** 7	**9.** 7	**10.** 3

Divide and Conquer 51

1. 54	**2.** 68	**3.** 83	circle: 205
4. 94	**5.** 58	**6.** 47	circle: 199
7. 20	**8.** 73	**9.** 21	circle: 114

Compare the Prices 52

Explanations will vary.
1. 12-ounce bottle
2. one 12 pack of soda
3. 16-ounce can of soup
4. 24-ounce bottle of water
5. one box of 12 soaps

Customary Length Units 54

1. miles	**2.** yards	**3.** feet	**4.** inches
5. feet	**6.** miles	**7.** inches	**8.** inches
9. feet	**10.** feet		

Power Practice: Students' problems will vary.

Convert Customary Units 55

1. 72 inches	**2.** 4 yards	**3.** 21,120 feet
4. 18 feet	**5.** 4 feet	**6.** 30 inches
7. 6 feet	**8.** 15,840 feet	**9.** $8\frac{1}{2}$ yards
10. $1\frac{1}{2}$ feet	**11.** $3\frac{1}{2}$ feet	

12. She will need to buy 7 rolls of ribbon. It will cost $17.43.

Power Practice: Students' word problems will vary.

Converting mm to cm 56

1. 3 cm	**2.** 9 cm	**3.** 6 cm
4. 14 cm	**5.** 1 cm	**6.** 16 cm
7. 11 cm	**8.** 5 cm	**9.** 18 cm
10. 13 cm	**11.** 8 cm	**12.** 19 cm
13. 4 cm	**14.** 12 cm	**15.** 20 cm

16. Answers will vary.

Finding Perimeter and Area 57

1. 36 feet	**2.** 36 feet	**3.** 35 feet
4. 20 square units	**5.** 9 square units	
6. 11 square units		

Perimeter Word Problems . . . . . . page 58

1. 120 in.
2. width = 14 ft., length = 28 ft.
3. 20 m
4. 16 m
5. 15 ft.

Power Practice: Students' story problems will vary.

Area of Triangles, Rectangles, and Parallelograms 59

1. 18	**2.** 16	**3.** 10	**4.** 50
5. 9	**6.** 9		

Using a Rule to Find Volume 60

1. height = 4, length = 3, width = 1, 12 cubic units
2. height = 2, length = 4, width = 4, 32 cubic units
3. height = 3, length = 3, width = 2, 18 cubic units
4. height = 3, length = 1, width = 2, 6 cubic units
5. height = 2, length = 5, width = 1, 10 cubic units

Answer Key

Volume of Prisms . . . . page 61
1. 48 cubic units
2. 96 cubic units
3. 81 cubic units
4. 250 cubic units
5. 816 cubic units
6. 2 x 3 x 4
7. 1 x 2 x 2
8. 3 x 4 x 5

Power Practice: To find the volume of a rectangular prism, multiply the length by the width by the height. You use different formulas for different shapes.

Angle Names . . . . page 62
1. 90°; right
2. 154°; obtuse
3. 48°; acute
4. 17°; acute
5. 180°; obtuse
6. 76°; acute
7. 99°; obtuse
8. 26°; acute

Angle Identification . . . . page 63
1. obtuse
2. acute
3. right
4. obtuse
5. acute
6. Clocks will vary.

Converting Units of Measurement 65
1. 1 gallon
2. 40 fl. oz.
3. 48 Tbs.
4. 4 quarts
5. 2 cups
6. 20 pints
7. 6 quarts
8. 4 quarts
9. 2 gallons
10. 6 Tbs.

Recipe Measuring . . . . page 66
1. no, 2 cups short
2. yes, exact amount
3. 2 cups/1 pint
4. yes, exact amount
5. no, 6 cups short
6. 2 quarts/8 cups

Customary Weight . . . . page 67
1. ton
2. pound
3. ounce
4. ton
5. ounce
6. pound
7. ounce
8. ounce
9. ton
10. pound

Power Practice: Students' examples will vary.

Matching Weights . . . . page 68
1. h or g
2. j
3. b
4. d
5. i
6. c
7. e
8. a
9. f
10. g or h
11. Answers will vary.

Metric Weight . . . . page 69
1. gram
2. kilogram
3. gram
4. gram
5. gram
6. kilogram
7. kilogram
8. kilogram
9. A kilogram is 1,000 grams.

Power Practice: Students' weights will vary. Check conversions from grams to kilograms.

Time in Numbers and Words . . . page 70
1. 1:15; one fifteen
2. 2:55; two fifty-five
3. 4:25; four twenty-five
4. 10:45; ten forty-five
5. 11:15; eleven fifteen
6. 5:30; five thirty

Power Practice: Students' answers will vary.

Time Word Problems 71
1. 35 minutes
2. 2:45 P.M.
3. two weeks (14 days)
4. April 3
5. 25 minutes

Time Conversions 72
1. 30 years
2. 365 days
3. 180 seconds
4. 12 hours
5. 14 days
6. 30 minutes
7. 90 seconds
8. 48 hours
9. 31 days
10. 40 years

Fahrenheit Temperature . . . . page 73
1. 34°F
2. 61°F
3. 101°F
4. 72°F
5. 65°F
6. 72°F
7. 42°F

Power Practice: Students' answers might vary slightly but should indicate that to convert Fahrenheit to Celsius you subtract 32 and then multiply by 5/9.

Fill in the Thermometer . . . . page 74
1. thermometer should show 20°C
2. thermometer should show 103°F
3. thermometer should show 30°F

Pattern Match-Up . . . . page 76
1. C
2. D
3. A
4. B

The Case of the Missing Numbers page 77
1. 3, 8, 13, 18, 23, 28, 33, 38; + 5
2. 50,000,000; 5,000,000; 500,000; 50,000; 5,000; 500; 50; ÷ 10
3. 722, 656, 590, 524, 458, 392, 326, 260; – 66
4. 1.25; 5; 20; 80; 320; 1,280; 5,120; 20,480; x 4

Power Practice: Students' answers will vary.

Answer Key

A Tidy Sum . . . . page 78
1. **a.** growing
    b. No. The amount of change is always different.
    c. Add the previous two numbers in the pattern.
    d. 97, 157, 254
2. **a.** decreasing
    b. No. The amount of change is always different.
    c. Subtract the previous two numbers in the pattern.
    d. 9, 6, 3

Power Practice: Both patterns are decreasing patterns, and they both do not decrease at a constant rate.

In and Out . . . . page 79

1.
IN	3	9	11	6	8
OUT	6	18	22	12	16

Rule: OUT = IN x 2

2.
IN	4	7	19	44	18
OUT	12	15	27	52	26

Rule: OUT = IN + 8

3.
IN	55	38	72	61	80
OUT	26	9	43	32	51

Rule: OUT = IN − 29

4.
IN	108	27	63	126	18
OUT	12	3	7	14	2

Rule: OUT = IN ÷ 9

Power Practice: Students' answers will vary.

Payment Plan 80
1–2. Answers may vary.
3–5. Estimates may vary.
6. Answers may vary.
7. 7th day = 64¢; 14th day = $81.92; 31st day = $10,737,418.24
8. It's a great deal!

A Sweet Treat . . . . page 81
1. B = # of candy bars the class ate
2. total # of candy bars − # of candy bars the class ate = # of candy bars left
3. 250 − B = 75
4. B = 175
5. The class ate 175 candy bars.

Alphabet Soup . . . . page 82
1. W = 2, Y = 6
2. B = 20, C = 4
3. K = 5, L = 10
4. M = 40, N = 18
5. D = 7, F = 18
6. P = 4, Q = 20
7. T = 3, V = 5
8. H = 16, J =25

Coordinate Graphing 83
1. acorn (2, 3)
2. frog (3, 3)
3. worm (5, 4)
4. lily pad (3, 5)
5. boat (6, 1)
6. picnic basket (4, 2)
7. rock (5, 7)
8. butterfly (0, 4)
9. flower (2, 6)
10. leaf (1, 7)
11. fish (1, 4)
12. bird (6, 6)

Picture Plots 84
1-3.

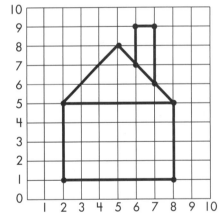

4. house

Answer Key

Making Money . . . . pages 85
1. $10; $15
2.

# of hours	1	2	3	4	5	6
amt. earned	5	10	15	20	25	30

3.
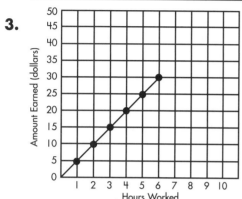

Lines, Line Segments and Rays 87
1. d   **2.** c   **3.** e   **4.** a   **5.** b

A Class by Itself 88
1. a. right scalene   **b.** obtuse isosceles
   c. acute scalene   **d.** acute equilateral
   e. obtuse scalene   **f.** right isosceles
   g. acute isosceles   **h.** acute scalene
   i. right isosceles

Describing Quadrilaterals 89
1. acute, unequal   **2.** right, unequal
3. acute, obtuse   **4.** equal, right
5. parallel
Power Practice: Answers will vary. Sample answer: A quadrilateral where each vertex is formed by perpendicular lines.

Pyramids and Prisms 90
1. prism   **2.** neither   **3.** pyramid
4. pyramid   **5.** prism   **6.** neither
7. prism   **8.** pyramid   **9.** prism

Classifying Prisms 91
1. Group 1: Circled shape has a pentagon for a base and others have rectangular bases.
Group 2: Circled shape has a hexagon for a base and others have triangular bases.
Group 3: Circled shape has rectangular base and others have hexagonal bases.
2. Group 1: Rectangular bases
Group 2: Triangular bases
Group 3: Hexagonal bases

Faces and Edges 92

	Number of Faces	Number of Edges	Number of Vertices	Shape(s) of Faces
1.	6	12	8	square
2.	6	12	8	rectangles
3.	5	9	6	triangles, squares or rectangles
4.	4	6	4	triangles
5.	5	8	5	triangles, square

Congruency and Symmetry 93
1. Congruent means same size and same shape.
2. Symmetry means that both of a shape's halves are congruent.
3. yes
4. Answers will vary.
5. Answers will vary.

Create Congruent Figures 94
Answers will vary.
Sample answers are shown.
1.
2.
3.
4.
5.

Answer Key

Lines of Symmetry. 95
1. 4 **2.** 6 **3.** 1

4. 8 **5.** 5 **6.** 2

Point Symmetry. 96
1. no **2.** yes **3.** yes **4.** no
5. yes **6.** yes

Pictograph. 98
1. 57 **2.** theater **3.** 12
4. no **5.** zoo

Line Plots. 99
1. 25 **2.** 4 **3.** 18 **4.** 7
Power Practice: 6

Make a Bar Graph 100
Graphs will vary. Sample graph is shown.

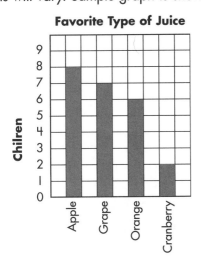

Favorite Type of Juice

Stem and Leaf Plots. 101
1. The stem shows all the digits except the digits in the ones place.
2. 52.2 minutes **3.** 29 minutes **4.** 100 minutes

Median, Mode, and Range 102
1. median = 15, mode = 14, range = 8
2. median = 53, mode = 52, range = 10
3. median = 12, mode = 14, range = 9
4. median = 82, mode = 82, range = 11

5. median = 73, mode = 73, range = 8
6. median = 4, mode = 4, range = 7
7. median = 34, mode = 36, range = 5
8. median = 25, mode = 25, range = 27

Means in the World. 103
1. 48.75 mph **2.** 1,438 feet
3. 251.2 feet **4.** 5,673 miles

Way Out There 104
1. 21 **2.** 5
Power Practice: yes; Explanations will vary, but may include that there could be an outlier on the greater end of data values and one on the lesser end of the data values.

Probability 105
1. pulling a red chip; $\frac{1}{2} > \frac{1}{4}$
2. rolling an odd number with both number cubes; $\frac{1}{4} > \frac{1}{6}$
3. peanut butter; There are more peanut butter cookies.
Power Practice: percents and decimals

Spinner Fun 106
1. red **2.** blue **3.** yellow, green, and orange
4. any color not red, blue, yellow, green, or orange
5. Answers will vary.
6. $\frac{5}{8}$ **7.** $\frac{3}{8}$ **8.** 1
9. 0 **10.** $\frac{2}{8} = \frac{1}{4}$ **11.** $\frac{1}{8}$
12. $\frac{2}{8} = \frac{1}{4}$

Pick a Card 107
1. $\frac{1}{7}$ **2.** $\frac{3}{7}$ **3.** $\frac{4}{7}$
4. $\frac{3}{7}$ **5.** $\frac{4}{7}$ **6.** $\frac{1}{7}$
Power Practice: Adding an "S" to create "OUTCOMES" makes the probability of picking a vowel and picking a consonant the same.

Answer Key

Find the Number 109
1. standard: 125,947, expanded: 100,000 + 20,000 + 5,000 + 900 + 40 + 7
2. standard: 35,393, expanded: 30,000 + 5,000 + 300 + 90 + 3
3. standard: 876,543, expanded: 800,000 + 70,000 + 6,000 + 500 + 40 + 3
4. standard: 555,444, expanded: 500,000 + 50,000 + 5,000 + 400 + 40 + 4
5. standard: 97,531, expanded: 90,000 + 7,000 + 500 + 30 + 1
6. standard: 543,986, expanded: 500,000 + 40,000 + 3,000 + 900 + 80 + 6

Choose Your Operation 110
1. subtract
2. divide
3. divide
4. multiply
5. add
6. multiply
7. divide
8. multiply
9. subtract
10. add

Power Practice:
1. $22.28
2. 347 students
3. 244 beads
4. $63.52
5. 754 students
6. $4.44
7. 15 pages
8. 54 scoops
9. 56 minutes
10. 362 quarters

Use Your Head 111
1. 75 + 50 = 125; yes, she has enough.
2. No. 26 + 24 + 25 = 75 students; however, if she and her brother and sister do not get one, there is enough since 75 − 3 = 72.
3. $3.52 + $0.84 + $1.44 = $5.80; not enough.
4. 57 + 107 + 230 + 61 = 455; not enough.
5. 26 + 26 = 52 students; 12 + 12 + 12 + 12 = 48; she needs one more package since 48 + 12 = 60.
6. 500 + 500 + 500 = 1,500 + 847 = 2,347; not enough, 500 + 500 + 500 + 500 = 2,000 + 847 = 2847. He needs 4 more boxes.

Addition Problem Solving 112
1. 1,054
2. 461
3. 1,419
4. 18 blocks
5. 15
6. Answers may vary.
   $12.00 + $6.00 + $6.00 = $24.00

Subtraction Problem Solving 113
Team One

	Sit-Ups	Push-Ups	Jumping Jacks	Meters Run
Total	91	82	83	1,500

Team Two

	Sit-Ups	Push-Ups	Jumping Jacks	Meters Run
Total	82	84	88	1,750

1. 18
2. 32
3. Team Two
4. Team Two

Multiplication Problem Solving 114
1. 48
2. 120
3. 36
4. 85
5. 60
6. $70.00

Multiple-Step Problems 115
1. 8
2. 6
3. 5
4. 22

Smart Shopper 116
1. a. $0.27   b. $5.22 ÷ 20 = $0.26,   c. 20
2. Oranges in the bag cost $0.14 each ($1.69 ÷ 12 = 0.14), which is cheaper than buying them separately.
3. Deshawn ($0.40 per card, rather than $0.50 per card)

Power Practice: Take the price for 12 oz. and divide by 12.

Riddles 117
1. 2 quarters, 5 dimes, 5 pennies
2. 3 fifty-cent pieces, 1 quarter, 1 dime, 1 nickel
3. 2 dimes, 3 nickels, 2 pennies
4. 2 fifty-cent pieces, 2 quarters, 4 dimes, 1 nickel, 5 pennies
5. 3 dimes, 5 pennies, 1 quarter
6. 2 fifty-cent pieces, 2 dimes, 2 nickels
7. 20 dimes
8. Answers will vary.

Money 118
1. $0.37 (3 dimes, 1 nickel, 2 pennies)
2. $1.90 (3 half-dollars, 2 dimes, 4 nickels)
3. $0.37 (1 quarter, 1 dime, 2 pennies)
4. $1.14 (2 half-dollars, 2 nickels, 4 pennies)
5. $1.92 (6 quarters, 4 dimes, 2 pennies)
6. $3.30 (5 half-dollars, 2 quarters, 3 dimes)